Virtual Reality and Society

A Case Study

Hassan Yamamoto

ISBN: 9781779666284
Imprint: Press for Play Books
Copyright © 2024 Hassan Yamamoto.
All Rights Reserved.

Contents

Introduction	1
The Rise of Virtual Reality	1
Virtual Reality and Society	27
Virtual Reality and Socialization	27
Bibliography	31
Bibliography	37
Virtual Reality and Ethics	54
Bibliography	77
Bibliography	81
Virtual Reality and Education	81
Bibliography	85
Bibliography	89
Virtual Reality and Healthcare	109
Bibliography	127
Bibliography	133
Bibliography	139
Virtual Reality and Entertainment	139
Bibliography	155

Bibliography	**165**
Case Studies	**167**
Virtual Reality in Education	167
Bibliography	**175**
Bibliography	**183**
Bibliography	**189**
Virtual Reality in Healthcare	194
Bibliography	**207**
Index	**223**

Introduction

The Rise of Virtual Reality

The Origins of Virtual Reality

The concept of Virtual Reality (VR) has its roots in the early explorations of immersive environments and simulation technologies. While the term "virtual reality" itself gained popularity in the 1980s, the underlying ideas can be traced back to earlier technological advancements and artistic expressions.

Early Concepts and Theoretical Foundations

The origins of VR can be linked to several pioneering works in computer graphics, simulation, and human-computer interaction. One of the earliest examples of a VR-like experience was the "Sensorama," developed by Morton Heilig in the 1960s. The Sensorama was a multi-sensory machine that provided users with a simulated experience of riding a motorcycle through the streets of Brooklyn. It combined 3D visuals, stereo sound, vibrations, and even scents to create a more immersive experience, laying the groundwork for future VR developments.

In the 1970s, computer scientist Ivan Sutherland developed the first head-mounted display (HMD) system known as the "Sword of Damocles." This device was a rudimentary prototype that allowed users to view simple wireframe graphics in a 3D space. Although it was heavy and cumbersome, Sutherland's work is often considered the birth of virtual reality technology. He famously stated, "The ultimate display would be a room within which the computer can control the existence of matter." This vision encapsulated the potential of VR to create entirely new worlds.

The Role of Gaming and Simulation

The gaming industry played a significant role in the evolution of VR technology. In the 1980s, the introduction of arcade games such as "Battlezone" utilized vector graphics to create a pseudo-3D experience. Players operated a tank in a simulated battlefield, and the immersive nature of the game drew attention to the potential for VR in entertainment.

Moreover, the development of flight simulators in the military further advanced VR technology. These simulators provided pilots with realistic training experiences, allowing them to practice maneuvers in a safe environment. The use of high-fidelity graphics and motion feedback systems demonstrated the effectiveness of VR in training and education.

Technological Advancements

The 1990s saw significant advancements in VR technology, fueled by the rise of personal computing and graphics processing capabilities. Companies like VPL Research and Virtuality began developing commercial VR systems, including gloves and suits that tracked user movements. However, despite the technological progress, the high costs and technical limitations of the time hindered widespread adoption.

The introduction of the Internet in the late 1990s opened new avenues for VR applications. Online multiplayer games and virtual worlds, such as "Second Life," emerged, allowing users to interact in shared virtual spaces. These platforms provided a glimpse into the social aspects of VR, demonstrating its potential for community building and interaction.

Challenges and Limitations

Despite the excitement surrounding VR, several challenges persisted. Early systems suffered from issues such as motion sickness, limited field of view, and low-resolution graphics. Users often experienced discomfort due to the disconnect between physical movement and visual feedback. This phenomenon, known as "cybersickness," posed a significant barrier to the adoption of VR technologies.

Furthermore, ethical considerations began to surface as VR gained traction. Questions regarding privacy, data security, and the potential for addiction became increasingly relevant. The immersive nature of VR raised concerns about users' ability to distinguish between virtual experiences and reality, leading to debates about the psychological impacts of prolonged VR exposure.

The Resurgence of Virtual Reality

The 21st century marked a resurgence in interest and investment in VR technology. The introduction of more affordable and accessible VR headsets, such as the Oculus Rift and HTC Vive, brought immersive experiences to a wider audience. Advances in graphics processing, motion tracking, and user interface design contributed to the development of more sophisticated VR applications.

Today, VR is not only a tool for entertainment but also a valuable resource in various fields, including education, healthcare, and social interaction. As technology continues to evolve, the origins of virtual reality serve as a reminder of the innovative spirit that drives the quest for immersive experiences.

Conclusion

The origins of virtual reality are rooted in a rich history of technological innovation, artistic exploration, and theoretical foundations. From the early experiments of Morton Heilig to the modern advancements in VR headsets, the journey of VR has been marked by both triumphs and challenges. As we continue to explore the potential of virtual reality, understanding its origins provides valuable insights into its future development and societal impact.

The Evolution of Virtual Reality Technology

The journey of Virtual Reality (VR) technology is a fascinating tale of innovation, creativity, and the relentless pursuit of immersive experiences. This section will explore the key milestones in the evolution of VR technology, highlighting significant advancements, challenges faced, and the implications of these developments on society.

Early Concepts and Prototypes

The concept of virtual reality can be traced back to the 1960s, with the creation of the *Sensorama*, an arcade-style theater invented by Morton Heilig. This device combined 3D visuals, sound, vibrations, and even smells to create a multi-sensory experience for users. Although it was not an interactive VR experience, it laid the groundwork for future developments by demonstrating the potential of immersive environments.

In 1968, Ivan Sutherland developed the first head-mounted display (HMD), often referred to as the *Sword of Damocles*. This primitive device was bulky and tethered to a computer, but it allowed users to view computer-generated graphics in a stereoscopic format. The limitations of hardware and computing power at the time hindered its practical use, but it marked a pivotal moment in VR history.

The 1980s and 1990s: The Birth of Commercial VR

The 1980s and 1990s saw a surge in interest and investment in virtual reality, particularly in the gaming and entertainment sectors. Companies like *VPL Research* developed gloves and suits that allowed users to interact with virtual environments, while *Virtuality Group* introduced arcade games that utilized VR technology. However, the high cost of equipment and the lack of compelling content limited widespread adoption.

In 1991, Sega announced the *Sega VR*, a headset designed for its gaming console. Although it never reached the market, it generated significant buzz and highlighted the growing interest in consumer VR. Similarly, Nintendo's *Virtual Boy*, released in 1995, attempted to bring VR to home gaming but was met with criticism due to its monochromatic display and lack of immersive gameplay.

Technological Challenges and Setbacks

Despite the excitement surrounding VR in the 1990s, several technological challenges hindered its progress. The limitations of graphics processing power, motion tracking accuracy, and display technology led to a phenomenon known as *VR sickness*, where users experienced nausea and disorientation. These issues, combined with the high costs associated with VR systems, resulted in a decline in interest and investment in the late 1990s and early 2000s.

The Resurgence of Virtual Reality

The resurgence of VR technology began in the early 2010s, fueled by advancements in computing power, display technology, and motion tracking. The introduction of the *Oculus Rift* in 2012, a Kickstarter-funded project, reignited interest in VR. The Rift's high-resolution display and precise motion tracking provided an immersive experience that was previously unattainable. This success prompted major tech companies, including Facebook, Sony, and HTC, to invest heavily in VR development.

The advent of mobile VR platforms, such as Google Cardboard and Samsung Gear VR, further democratized access to virtual reality. These affordable solutions allowed users to experience VR using their smartphones, significantly expanding the user base and paving the way for innovative applications across various fields.

Current State of VR Technology

Today, VR technology has evolved to include a wide range of applications beyond gaming and entertainment. In education, immersive simulations allow students to engage with complex concepts in a hands-on manner. In healthcare, VR is being utilized for pain management, rehabilitation, and surgical training. The gaming industry has also embraced VR, with titles that offer rich storytelling and interactive gameplay experiences.

Despite these advancements, challenges remain. Issues related to data privacy, accessibility, and the potential for addiction continue to be areas of concern. The ethical implications of VR technology, particularly in relation to emotional manipulation and the distortion of reality, require careful consideration as the technology becomes more integrated into everyday life.

The Future of VR Technology

Looking ahead, the future of virtual reality technology appears promising. Continued advancements in artificial intelligence, haptic feedback, and wireless technology are expected to enhance the immersive experience further. The development of the *metaverse*, a collective virtual shared space, presents new opportunities for social interaction, commerce, and creative expression.

As VR technology continues to evolve, it is crucial to address the ethical considerations and societal impacts associated with its use. Ensuring that VR remains an inclusive and accessible medium will be essential for fostering positive experiences and outcomes for all users.

In conclusion, the evolution of virtual reality technology is a testament to human ingenuity and the desire to explore new frontiers. From its humble beginnings to its current state as a transformative tool across various sectors, VR technology has the potential to reshape our understanding of reality and enhance our interactions with the world around us.

The Impact of Virtual Reality on Entertainment

Virtual Reality (VR) has revolutionized the entertainment industry, creating immersive experiences that engage users in ways previously unimaginable. The impact of VR on entertainment can be examined through various lenses, including technological advancements, user engagement, and the evolution of content creation. This section delves into these aspects while addressing the challenges and ethical considerations that accompany this rapidly evolving medium.

Technological Advancements

The development of VR technology has significantly enhanced the entertainment landscape. High-definition displays, spatial audio, and motion tracking systems allow users to experience environments that feel real. For instance, the Oculus Rift and HTC Vive have set new standards for VR gaming, providing users with a sense of presence that traditional gaming cannot match. The equation that often describes user immersion in VR environments can be represented as:

$$I = f(T, E, S) \tag{1}$$

where I is the level of immersion, T is the technology used, E is the emotional engagement of the user, and S represents the sensory feedback provided by the VR system.

As technology continues to advance, the quality of VR experiences is expected to improve further. The integration of artificial intelligence (AI) into VR experiences can personalize content, adapting to user preferences and behaviors. For example, AI can analyze user interactions to create tailored storylines in VR narratives, enhancing engagement and replayability.

User Engagement

User engagement in VR is markedly different from traditional media. In VR, users are not passive observers; they actively participate in the experience. This shift in engagement has profound implications for storytelling and content consumption. For instance, VR experiences like *The Walking Dead: Saints & Sinners* allow players to make choices that affect the narrative, creating a sense of agency that is often lacking in conventional video games.

Research indicates that the level of interactivity in VR can enhance emotional responses. A study by [?] found that users who interacted with VR environments reported higher levels of emotional arousal compared to those who viewed non-interactive content. This emotional connection can lead to a deeper investment in the narrative and characters, resulting in a more memorable experience.

Challenges and Ethical Considerations

While the impact of VR on entertainment is largely positive, it is not without challenges. One significant issue is the potential for addiction. The immersive nature of VR can lead to prolonged use, causing users to neglect real-world responsibilities. As noted by [?], excessive gaming can lead to negative psychological effects, including anxiety and depression.

Moreover, ethical considerations surrounding VR content must be addressed. The potential for emotional manipulation in VR experiences raises questions about the responsibility of developers. For example, VR horror games can induce extreme fear and anxiety, leading to discussions about the ethical implications of such experiences. The equation representing the potential emotional impact can be expressed as:

$$E = g(I, C) \qquad (2)$$

where E is the emotional impact, I is the level of immersion, and C represents the content's nature (e.g., horror, drama). Developers must navigate these ethical waters carefully to ensure that they create experiences that are enjoyable without crossing into harmful territory.

Examples of VR in Entertainment

Numerous examples illustrate the transformative power of VR in entertainment. One notable instance is the use of VR in theme parks. Parks like Universal Studios and Disneyland have incorporated VR rides that transport users into fantastical worlds, enhancing the thrill of traditional amusement rides. The *Harry Potter and the Forbidden Journey* ride, for example, combines physical motion with VR elements to create an unparalleled experience.

In the realm of film, VR has begun to redefine storytelling. Projects like *The Invisible Man* have explored how VR can create immersive narratives that allow viewers to experience the story from different perspectives. This innovation opens up new avenues for filmmakers to engage audiences and tell stories in ways that traditional cinema cannot.

Conclusion

The impact of Virtual Reality on entertainment is profound and multifaceted. As technology continues to evolve, the potential for VR to create engaging, immersive experiences will only grow. However, it is essential to address the challenges and ethical considerations that accompany this medium to ensure that VR remains a positive force in entertainment. By balancing innovation with responsibility, the entertainment industry can harness the full potential of VR to captivate audiences in new and exciting ways.

Virtual Reality and the Gaming Industry

The gaming industry has been at the forefront of adopting and innovating virtual reality (VR) technologies. With the advent of more powerful hardware and sophisticated software, VR has transformed the gaming landscape, offering immersive experiences that traditional gaming platforms cannot match. This section explores the synergy between virtual reality and gaming, examining its theoretical foundations, challenges, and notable examples.

Theoretical Foundations

At its core, the integration of virtual reality in gaming can be understood through the lens of immersion and presence. Immersion refers to the degree to which a player feels enveloped in a virtual environment, while presence is the psychological state of being in that environment. Both concepts are crucial for enhancing player engagement and satisfaction.

$$\text{Immersion} = \frac{\text{Sensory Input}}{\text{Distraction}} \qquad (3)$$

Where sensory input includes visual, auditory, and haptic feedback, and distraction refers to external stimuli that can pull the player out of the experience.

Challenges in the VR Gaming Industry

Despite its potential, the adoption of VR in gaming faces several challenges:

- **Hardware Limitations:** High-quality VR experiences often require expensive headsets and powerful computers, which can limit accessibility for many gamers. For instance, while the Oculus Rift and HTC Vive offer excellent experiences, their price points can be prohibitive.

- **Motion Sickness:** Many players experience motion sickness when using VR, which can be attributed to a disconnect between visual motion and physical movement. This phenomenon, known as *cybersickness*, poses a significant barrier to widespread adoption.

- **Content Creation:** Developing engaging VR content is resource-intensive. Game developers must consider not only the gameplay mechanics but also how to create an immersive environment that feels alive and responsive.

- **Social Interaction:** While VR can enhance social experiences in gaming, it also raises concerns about isolation. Players may find themselves physically alone while engaging with others in a virtual space, leading to a paradox of connectivity versus loneliness.

Notable Examples of VR in Gaming

Several games and platforms have successfully harnessed VR technology, showcasing its potential:

- **Beat Saber:** This rhythm game has gained immense popularity for its engaging gameplay, where players slash blocks representing musical beats with lightsabers. The combination of music, movement, and VR creates an exhilarating experience that keeps players coming back.

- **Half-Life: Alyx:** As a flagship VR title from Valve, *Half-Life: Alyx* demonstrates the narrative potential of VR gaming. Players navigate a richly detailed world, solving puzzles and engaging in combat, all while feeling a sense of presence that traditional games struggle to achieve.

- **Rec Room:** This social VR platform allows players to interact in a virtual space, play games, and create content collaboratively. It exemplifies how VR can foster community and social interaction, bridging the gap between physical and virtual worlds.

- **VRChat:** Similar to *Rec Room*, *VRChat* offers a space for users to create avatars, socialize, and participate in a variety of user-generated games and activities. It highlights the importance of user-generated content in the VR gaming landscape.

The Future of VR in Gaming

Looking ahead, the future of virtual reality in the gaming industry appears promising yet complex. As technology advances, we can expect improvements in hardware affordability, software development, and user experience. The potential for VR to create more inclusive gaming experiences is also worth noting, particularly for individuals with disabilities.

Moreover, the development of cross-platform VR experiences could bridge the gap between traditional and virtual gaming, allowing for a more cohesive gaming community. The integration of augmented reality (AR) with VR may further enhance gameplay, creating hybrid experiences that blend the physical and digital worlds.

In conclusion, virtual reality has the potential to redefine the gaming industry. While challenges remain, the ongoing evolution of technology and content creation will likely lead to more immersive, engaging, and inclusive gaming experiences in the future. As we navigate this exciting frontier, the interplay between virtual reality and gaming will continue to shape our understanding of entertainment and social interaction in the digital age.

Virtual Reality as a Tool for Education

Virtual Reality (VR) has emerged as a transformative tool in education, providing immersive experiences that enhance learning outcomes. This section explores the theoretical foundations, challenges, and practical applications of VR in educational settings.

Theoretical Foundations

The use of VR in education is grounded in several educational theories, including constructivism, experiential learning, and situated learning.

- **Constructivism** posits that learners construct knowledge through experiences. VR environments allow students to engage actively with content, facilitating deeper understanding.

- **Experiential Learning**, articulated by Kolb (1984), emphasizes learning through experience. VR simulations provide students with hands-on experiences that would be difficult or impossible to replicate in a traditional classroom.

- **Situated Learning** suggests that knowledge is best acquired in context. VR can create authentic learning environments that situate students in real-world scenarios, enhancing relevance and retention.

Advantages of VR in Education

The integration of VR in educational contexts offers several advantages:

1. **Enhanced Engagement:** VR captures students' attention and motivates them through interactive experiences. Research indicates that students in

VR environments report higher levels of engagement compared to traditional learning methods [?].

2. **Personalized Learning:** VR can cater to diverse learning styles and paces, allowing students to explore content at their own speed. For instance, platforms like ClassVR enable teachers to customize VR lessons based on individual student needs.

3. **Safe Learning Environments:** VR allows for the simulation of dangerous or complex scenarios without real-world risks. Medical students can practice surgeries in a VR setting, gaining experience without jeopardizing patient safety.

4. **Increased Retention:** Studies suggest that immersive experiences lead to better information retention. According to a study by Mikropoulos and Natsis (2011), students who engaged in VR learning retained information longer than those who learned through traditional methods.

Challenges of Implementing VR in Education

Despite its potential, the implementation of VR in education is not without challenges:

- **Cost:** The financial investment required for VR hardware and software can be prohibitive for many educational institutions. Schools must consider budget constraints and seek funding opportunities to integrate VR effectively.

- **Technical Issues:** VR technology can be complex and may require significant technical support. Educators must be adequately trained to troubleshoot issues and effectively integrate VR into their curricula.

- **Accessibility:** Not all students have equal access to VR technology, which can exacerbate the digital divide. Schools must ensure that all students have the opportunity to benefit from VR experiences.

- **Content Development:** There is a limited amount of high-quality educational VR content available. Educators may need to invest time in developing custom VR experiences tailored to their curriculum.

Examples of VR in Education

Several successful implementations of VR in education illustrate its potential:

- **Google Expeditions:** This platform allows teachers to take students on virtual field trips to historical sites, underwater reefs, and even outer space. Students can explore environments that would be logistically impossible to visit in person.

- **Labster:** Labster offers virtual science labs where students can conduct experiments in a safe, controlled environment. This platform is particularly beneficial for students in remote areas who may lack access to physical lab facilities.

- **zSpace:** zSpace combines VR and augmented reality (AR) to create interactive 3D learning experiences. Students can manipulate 3D models in subjects like biology and physics, enhancing their understanding of complex concepts.

Future Directions

The future of VR in education looks promising. As technology continues to advance, we can expect more affordable and accessible VR solutions. Furthermore, the integration of artificial intelligence (AI) with VR may lead to personalized learning experiences that adapt to individual student needs in real-time.

In conclusion, VR has the potential to revolutionize education by providing immersive, engaging, and personalized learning experiences. While challenges remain, ongoing research and technological advancements will likely address these issues, paving the way for broader adoption of VR in educational settings.

Virtual Reality in Healthcare

Virtual Reality (VR) has emerged as a transformative technology in the field of healthcare, providing innovative solutions for various medical applications. This section will explore the theoretical foundations of VR in healthcare, the problems it addresses, and practical examples of its implementation.

Theoretical Foundations

The integration of VR in healthcare is grounded in several psychological and physiological theories. One key theory is the **Embodiment Theory**, which posits that individuals can experience a sense of presence and agency within a virtual environment. This theory is crucial for understanding how patients can engage with VR simulations to alter their perceptions of pain, anxiety, and other medical conditions.

Another relevant framework is the **Cognitive Behavioral Theory (CBT)**, which emphasizes the role of thoughts and beliefs in emotional and behavioral responses. VR can simulate environments that help patients confront their fears or anxieties, making it a valuable tool in therapeutic settings.

Problems Addressed by VR in Healthcare

VR addresses several critical challenges in healthcare:

- **Pain Management:** Traditional pain management strategies often rely on medication, which can lead to dependency or side effects. VR provides a non-pharmacological alternative by immersing patients in engaging environments that distract them from pain.

- **Rehabilitation:** Physical rehabilitation can be tedious and demotivating for patients. VR can gamify rehabilitation exercises, making them more enjoyable and encouraging adherence to treatment regimens.

- **Surgical Training:** Surgical procedures require extensive training and practice. VR simulators allow medical professionals to practice complex procedures in a risk-free environment, enhancing their skills without compromising patient safety.

- **Mental Health Treatment:** Conditions such as PTSD, phobias, and anxiety disorders can be challenging to treat. VR exposure therapy allows patients to confront their fears in a controlled setting, facilitating gradual desensitization.

- **Patient Education:** Understanding medical procedures can be daunting for patients. VR can provide immersive educational experiences, helping patients visualize and comprehend their medical conditions and treatment options.

Practical Examples

Several studies and real-world applications illustrate the effectiveness of VR in healthcare:

Pain Management A study conducted by [?] demonstrated that patients undergoing painful procedures, such as burn wound care, reported significantly lower pain levels when using VR. The immersive experience of exploring a virtual world, such as a serene beach or a vibrant underwater scene, provided a distraction that reduced their perception of pain.

Rehabilitation The use of VR in rehabilitation is exemplified by the **Virtual Reality Rehabilitation System (VRRS)**, which has been employed in stroke recovery programs. Patients perform exercises in a virtual environment that adapts to their progress, providing real-time feedback and motivation. Research by [?] showed that patients using VR for rehabilitation had improved outcomes compared to traditional methods.

Surgical Training The **Osso VR** platform is a notable example of VR in surgical training. It offers a comprehensive library of surgical procedures that trainees can practice in a virtual environment. A study by [?] found that surgical residents who trained with VR simulations demonstrated better skills and confidence during actual surgeries compared to those who did not use VR.

Mental Health Treatment VR exposure therapy has been effectively utilized in treating phobias. For instance, patients with a fear of heights can experience virtual heights in a safe setting, allowing them to confront and manage their fear. Research by [?] highlighted the success of VR therapy in reducing anxiety levels in patients with specific phobias.

Patient Education VR has also been leveraged for patient education, particularly in pre-operative settings. The **VR Patient Education Program** developed at Stanford University allows patients to experience a virtual tour of their surgical procedure, enhancing their understanding and reducing pre-operative anxiety. A study by [?] found that patients who participated in VR education reported higher satisfaction and lower anxiety compared to those who received traditional education materials.

Conclusion

The integration of Virtual Reality in healthcare represents a significant advancement in the way medical professionals approach treatment, training, and patient care. By addressing critical challenges such as pain management, rehabilitation, surgical training, mental health treatment, and patient education, VR is reshaping the landscape of healthcare delivery. As technology continues to evolve, the potential applications of VR in healthcare will likely expand, offering even more innovative solutions to improve patient outcomes and experiences.

Virtual Reality in Social Interaction

Virtual reality (VR) has emerged as a transformative medium for social interaction, enabling individuals to connect in ways previously unimaginable. Unlike traditional social media platforms that often rely on text and images, VR allows users to engage in immersive, three-dimensional environments where they can interact with others in real-time. This section explores the dynamics of social interaction within VR, examining its impact on communication, relationships, and community building.

The Nature of Communication in VR

Communication in virtual environments is multifaceted, involving verbal, non-verbal, and contextual cues. The presence of avatars—digital representations of users—allows for a unique form of self-expression. Users can customize their avatars to reflect their identities, which can enhance social presence and intimacy. According to [?], the ability to embody an avatar can lead to increased empathy and understanding among users, as they experience interactions through the lens of another's identity.

However, VR communication is not without its challenges. The absence of physical cues, such as body language and facial expressions, can lead to misunderstandings. Research by [3] indicates that while avatars can convey emotions through gestures and movements, the fidelity of these representations can significantly affect the quality of interaction. Low-quality avatars may hinder effective communication, leading to feelings of disconnection or frustration.

Building and Maintaining Relationships

The potential for relationship building in VR is significant. Users can form bonds through shared experiences in virtual spaces, such as attending concerts, exploring worlds, or collaborating on projects. The immersive nature of VR fosters a sense of presence, making interactions feel more genuine. A study by [?] found that participants who engaged in VR interactions reported higher levels of trust and connection compared to those who interacted through traditional digital means.

Nonetheless, maintaining relationships in VR presents unique challenges. The transient nature of virtual environments can lead to a lack of continuity in interactions. Users may find it difficult to reconnect with friends or maintain ongoing conversations, as VR spaces often lack the permanence of social media platforms. Furthermore, the potential for addiction to VR experiences can strain real-world relationships, as individuals may prioritize virtual interactions over face-to-face connections [?].

Combatting Loneliness and Isolation

One of the most compelling applications of VR in social interaction is its potential to combat loneliness and social isolation. For individuals who struggle with social anxiety or mobility issues, VR can offer a safe and accessible space to connect with others. Programs like VRChat and AltspaceVR provide platforms for users to meet, socialize, and participate in events without the pressures of the physical world.

Research by [?] indicates that VR can significantly reduce feelings of loneliness, particularly among older adults. Participants in VR social programs reported increased feelings of belonging and community, highlighting the technology's potential to foster social connections. However, it is essential to recognize that VR is not a panacea for loneliness. While it can facilitate interactions, it may not replace the depth and richness of in-person relationships.

Social Media Integration and Virtual Communities

The integration of social media with VR platforms has further enhanced social interaction. Users can share their virtual experiences on platforms like Facebook and Twitter, expanding their social circles beyond the confines of the virtual world. This cross-platform interaction allows for a richer exchange of ideas and experiences, fostering a sense of community among users.

Moreover, virtual communities have emerged around shared interests, from gaming to art to activism. These communities provide a space for individuals to connect, collaborate, and support one another. For example, the virtual reality platform Rec Room has become a hub for users to create games, host events, and engage in discussions, demonstrating the potential of VR to cultivate vibrant online communities.

The Digital Divide and Cultural Exchange

Despite the promising aspects of VR in social interaction, it is crucial to address the digital divide that exists in accessing this technology. Not everyone has equal access to VR devices and high-speed internet, which can exacerbate existing social inequalities. As noted by [?], the lack of access can hinder individuals from participating in virtual communities, limiting their opportunities for social interaction.

On the other hand, VR has the potential to facilitate cultural exchange by connecting individuals from diverse backgrounds. Virtual environments can serve as platforms for cross-cultural dialogue, allowing users to share their experiences and perspectives. For instance, VR experiences that simulate cultural festivals or historical events can promote understanding and appreciation of different cultures, fostering empathy among users.

The Future of Social Interaction in VR

As VR technology continues to evolve, the possibilities for social interaction will expand. Innovations in haptic feedback, eye-tracking, and artificial intelligence may enhance the realism of interactions, making virtual socialization even more engaging. However, ethical considerations must guide the development of these technologies. Issues such as privacy, consent, and the potential for emotional manipulation must be addressed to ensure that VR remains a safe and inclusive space for social interaction.

In conclusion, virtual reality presents a unique landscape for social interaction, offering opportunities for connection, relationship building, and cultural exchange. While challenges exist, the potential for VR to enhance social experiences is immense. As we navigate the complexities of virtual socialization, it is essential to remain mindful of the ethical implications and strive for inclusivity in this evolving digital frontier.

The Psychological Effects of Virtual Reality

Virtual Reality (VR) has emerged as a transformative technology, offering immersive experiences that can significantly affect users' psychological states. This section explores the various psychological effects of VR, including its potential benefits and drawbacks, supported by relevant theories and examples.

Theoretical Framework

The psychological effects of VR can be understood through several theoretical lenses:

- **Presence Theory:** This theory posits that the more a user feels present in a virtual environment, the more likely they are to experience emotional and psychological responses similar to those in the real world. [?] Presence is a key factor in determining the effectiveness of VR experiences, particularly in therapeutic and educational contexts.

- **Social Presence Theory:** This theory extends the concept of presence to social interactions in VR. It suggests that users can experience a sense of social presence with others in the virtual world, which can enhance feelings of connection and empathy [?].

- **Cognitive Dissonance Theory:** This psychological theory explains the discomfort experienced when holding conflicting beliefs or attitudes. VR can create scenarios that challenge users' beliefs, leading to cognitive dissonance and, potentially, behavior change [?].

Positive Psychological Effects

VR has been shown to have several positive psychological effects, particularly in therapeutic settings:

- **Anxiety Reduction:** VR has been successfully used to treat anxiety disorders, including phobias and post-traumatic stress disorder (PTSD). For example, exposure therapy using VR allows patients to confront their fears in a controlled environment, leading to desensitization and reduced anxiety levels [?].

- **Empathy Building:** VR experiences can foster empathy by allowing users to embody different perspectives. Programs like *The Empathy Machine* place users in the shoes of marginalized individuals, promoting understanding and compassion [?].

- **Enhanced Learning:** Immersive VR environments can lead to improved engagement and retention of information. Studies have shown that students who learn in VR settings outperform their peers in traditional classrooms, likely due to the emotional and cognitive engagement facilitated by the medium [?].

Negative Psychological Effects

Despite its potential benefits, VR can also lead to negative psychological outcomes:

- **Disorientation and Motion Sickness:** Users may experience disorientation, nausea, or motion sickness due to the disconnect between visual stimuli and physical movement. This phenomenon, often referred to as *VR sickness*, can detract from the immersive experience and lead to negative associations with VR technology [?].

- **Desensitization to Violence:** Exposure to violent content in VR can desensitize users to real-world violence. Studies have shown that individuals who engage with violent VR games may exhibit increased aggression and reduced empathy toward others [?].

- **Addiction and Escapism:** The immersive nature of VR can lead to excessive use, where individuals may prefer virtual experiences over real-life interactions. This can result in social isolation and a decline in mental health, as users escape into virtual worlds to avoid confronting real-life challenges [2].

Case Studies and Examples

Several case studies illustrate the psychological effects of VR:

- **PTSD Treatment:** The use of VR in treating PTSD has gained traction, with programs like *Bravemind* allowing veterans to relive traumatic experiences in a safe environment. Research indicates significant reductions in PTSD symptoms following VR therapy sessions [?].

- **Empathy Training:** A notable example of empathy training through VR is the *Walk a Mile in My Shoes* project, which allows users to experience life from the perspective of a homeless individual. Participants reported increased empathy and a desire to engage in social activism following the experience [?].

- **Education and Skill Development:** VR has been implemented in medical training, providing students with realistic simulations of surgical procedures. This immersive learning environment enhances skill acquisition and boosts confidence in real-life scenarios [?].

Conclusion

The psychological effects of virtual reality are multifaceted, encompassing both positive and negative outcomes. While VR offers promising applications in therapy, education, and empathy building, it also poses risks related to disorientation, addiction, and desensitization. As VR technology continues to evolve, it is crucial for developers, educators, and mental health professionals to consider these psychological effects to harness its potential while mitigating adverse consequences.

Ethical Considerations in Virtual Reality Development

The rapid evolution of Virtual Reality (VR) technology has raised numerous ethical considerations that developers, users, and society must address. The immersive nature of VR creates unique challenges that necessitate careful examination to ensure that the technology is used responsibly and ethically.

Privacy Concerns

One of the most pressing ethical issues in VR development is privacy. VR systems often collect vast amounts of personal data, including biometric information, behavioral patterns, and social interactions. The potential for misuse of this data is significant. For instance, VR platforms might track users' movements and reactions, which can be exploited for targeted advertising or even psychological manipulation.

$$D = \int_{t_0}^{t_f} (\text{Data Collected})\, dt \qquad (4)$$

Where D represents the total data collected over the time interval from t_0 to t_f. Developers must implement stringent data protection measures, ensuring compliance with regulations such as the General Data Protection Regulation (GDPR) in the EU.

Data Security

Alongside privacy, data security is a critical concern. VR systems are vulnerable to hacking and data breaches, which can lead to unauthorized access to sensitive user information. For example, a breach in a VR gaming platform could expose personal details of users, leading to identity theft or harassment. Developers must prioritize robust security protocols, including encryption and secure user authentication methods, to safeguard user data.

Addiction

The immersive experience of VR can lead to addictive behaviors. Users may find themselves spending excessive amounts of time in virtual environments, neglecting their real-world responsibilities and relationships. This phenomenon is particularly concerning among younger audiences, who may struggle to distinguish between virtual experiences and reality. The World Health Organization has recognized gaming disorder as a mental health condition, highlighting the need for developers to design VR experiences that promote healthy usage patterns.

Distortion of Reality

VR has the potential to distort users' perceptions of reality. Prolonged exposure to virtual environments can lead to desensitization to real-world issues or create unrealistic expectations about social interactions and relationships. For instance, individuals who engage in VR simulations of violence may develop a diminished sensitivity to real-life violence, raising ethical questions about the content being created and consumed in VR.

Emotional Manipulation

The emotional impact of VR experiences can be profound. Developers have the power to design experiences that elicit strong emotional responses, which can be used for both positive and negative purposes. For example, VR can be used in therapeutic settings to help individuals confront phobias or traumatic experiences. However, there is a risk that developers could exploit these emotional triggers for commercial gain, leading to manipulative practices that prioritize profit over user welfare.

Ethical Dilemmas

The creation of virtual environments presents several ethical dilemmas. For instance, the depiction of violence, sexual content, or other sensitive subjects in VR raises questions about morality and responsibility. Developers must consider the potential impact of their content on users and society at large. The ethical principle of *do no harm* should guide the creation of VR experiences, ensuring that they do not perpetuate harmful stereotypes or contribute to societal issues such as violence or discrimination.

Regulation and Oversight

The lack of comprehensive regulation in the VR industry poses a significant ethical challenge. Unlike traditional media, which is often subject to strict guidelines, VR development operates in a relatively unregulated space. This absence of oversight can lead to unethical practices, such as the exploitation of vulnerable populations or the promotion of harmful content. Stakeholders, including developers, policymakers, and advocacy groups, must collaborate to establish ethical guidelines and regulatory frameworks that protect users and promote responsible VR development.

Gender Equality

Gender representation in VR content and development teams is another ethical consideration. The VR industry has been criticized for its lack of diversity, particularly in terms of gender. This imbalance can lead to the creation of experiences that do not accurately reflect the perspectives and experiences of all users. Developers should strive for inclusivity, ensuring that diverse voices are represented in both the creation of VR content and the teams behind the technology.

Accessibility

Accessibility in VR is a crucial ethical issue. Many VR experiences are not designed with individuals with disabilities in mind, limiting their access to this emerging technology. Developers have a responsibility to create inclusive experiences that accommodate users with varying abilities, ensuring that VR can be enjoyed by a diverse audience.

Discrimination

Finally, VR can inadvertently reinforce societal biases and discrimination. If developers are not mindful of the content they create, they may perpetuate harmful stereotypes or exclude certain groups from the narrative. Ethical VR development requires a commitment to inclusivity and an awareness of the potential impact of virtual experiences on societal attitudes and behaviors.

In conclusion, the ethical considerations in VR development are multifaceted and complex. As the technology continues to evolve, it is imperative that developers, users, and society engage in ongoing discussions about the ethical implications of VR. By prioritizing privacy, security, inclusivity, and responsible content creation, the VR industry can harness its potential for positive impact while mitigating the risks associated with this powerful technology.

The Future of Virtual Reality

The future of Virtual Reality (VR) holds immense potential, promising to transform various aspects of life, from entertainment to education, and even

THE RISE OF VIRTUAL REALITY

healthcare. As technology continues to evolve, we find ourselves standing on the brink of unprecedented advancements in immersive experiences. This section explores the anticipated developments in VR, the challenges that lie ahead, and the implications for society.

Technological Advancements

The future of VR technology is expected to be shaped by several key advancements:

- **Increased Accessibility:** As hardware becomes more affordable and widespread, VR is expected to become a common tool in households, schools, and workplaces. The proliferation of mobile VR devices and standalone headsets will allow more users to experience immersive environments without the need for high-end computers.

- **Improved Graphics and Realism:** Advancements in graphics processing units (GPUs) and rendering techniques will enhance the visual fidelity of VR environments. Technologies such as ray tracing and photorealistic rendering will create experiences that are indistinguishable from reality, allowing users to engage in hyper-realistic simulations.

- **Haptic Feedback and Sensory Integration:** The integration of haptic feedback devices will create more immersive experiences by simulating touch and interaction. Future VR systems may incorporate olfactory and gustatory stimuli, providing a multi-sensory experience that further blurs the line between virtual and real environments.

- **Artificial Intelligence:** AI will play a crucial role in personalizing VR experiences. Intelligent algorithms can analyze user behavior and preferences, adapting environments and scenarios to enhance engagement. AI-driven characters and avatars will provide more realistic interactions, making virtual worlds feel alive.

Potential Applications

The applications of VR are vast and varied, and their future development will likely lead to innovative uses across different sectors:

- **Education:** VR is poised to revolutionize education by providing immersive learning experiences. Students can explore historical events, conduct scientific experiments, or practice skills in safe, controlled environments. For example, medical students can perform virtual surgeries, gaining hands-on experience without the risks associated with real-life procedures.

- **Healthcare:** VR's potential in healthcare extends beyond training. It can be utilized for pain management, rehabilitation, and mental health treatment. For instance, patients undergoing physical therapy can engage in VR exercises that make rehabilitation more enjoyable and effective.

- **Workplace Training:** Companies will increasingly adopt VR for employee training, allowing for realistic simulations of job tasks. This can be particularly beneficial in high-risk industries, such as aviation and construction, where hands-on experience is crucial for safety.

- **Social Interaction:** As VR technology advances, virtual social spaces will become more prevalent. Users will be able to meet, collaborate, and socialize in immersive environments, potentially reducing feelings of loneliness and isolation. Platforms like VRChat are already paving the way for social interactions in virtual spaces.

Challenges Ahead

Despite the promising future of VR, several challenges must be addressed:

- **Privacy and Security:** As VR systems collect vast amounts of data, including biometric information and user behavior, concerns regarding privacy and data security will intensify. Ensuring the protection of users' personal information will be paramount to fostering trust in VR technologies.

- **Health Concerns:** Prolonged use of VR can lead to physical discomfort, including motion sickness and eye strain. As VR becomes more integrated into daily life, addressing these health concerns will be critical to user well-being.

- **Ethical Considerations:** The immersive nature of VR raises ethical questions, particularly regarding content creation and user manipulation. Developers must navigate the fine line between engaging experiences and potential emotional manipulation or exploitation.

- **Digital Divide:** As with many technologies, there is a risk that VR could exacerbate existing inequalities. Ensuring equitable access to VR technology will be essential to prevent a widening digital divide.

Conclusion

The future of Virtual Reality is bright, teeming with possibilities that could reshape how we learn, interact, and experience the world. As we stand on the cusp of this technological revolution, it is crucial to approach these advancements with a balanced perspective, recognizing both the potential benefits and the challenges that lie ahead. By fostering responsible development and equitable access, we can harness the power of VR to enhance our lives and build a more connected society.

$$E = mc^2 \tag{5}$$

Where E represents the energy of VR experiences, m symbolizes the mass of user engagement, and c is the speed of technological advancement. As we continue to innovate, the equation encapsulates the relationship between immersive experiences and their impact on society.

Virtual Reality and Society

Virtual Reality and Socialization

The Effects of Virtual Reality on Communication

Virtual Reality (VR) has emerged as a transformative medium that reshapes how individuals communicate, interact, and form relationships. This section explores the multifaceted effects of VR on communication, highlighting both the opportunities and challenges it presents.

Theoretical Framework

To understand the impact of VR on communication, we can reference the **Media Richness Theory**, which posits that different communication media vary in their ability to convey information effectively. According to this theory, richer media (like VR) can facilitate better understanding and emotional connection compared to leaner media (like text-based communication).

The richness of VR is characterized by its ability to simulate real-world interactions through immersive environments, allowing users to experience a sense of presence that traditional media cannot provide. This presence can enhance social cues, such as body language and eye contact, which are critical for effective communication.

Enhanced Communication Capabilities

One of the primary effects of VR on communication is the enhancement of non-verbal communication. In a virtual environment, users can engage in eye contact, gestures, and spatial orientation, which are integral to conveying emotions and intentions. For example, a study by [1] found that participants in VR interactions were more likely to perceive empathy and connection when they could see and interact with lifelike avatars.

Furthermore, VR enables individuals to communicate across geographical barriers, fostering global collaboration. For instance, companies like *Spatial* and *Mozilla Hubs* have developed platforms that allow remote teams to meet in virtual spaces, simulating the experience of being in the same room, thus enhancing team dynamics and creativity.

Challenges in VR Communication

Despite its advantages, VR communication also presents several challenges. One significant issue is the **digital divide**, which refers to the disparity in access to technology. Not everyone has the resources to engage in VR, leading to potential exclusion from important social interactions and collaborations.

Moreover, the immersive nature of VR can lead to **disassociation** from the real world. Users may become so engrossed in virtual interactions that they neglect face-to-face communication. This phenomenon is particularly concerning for younger generations who may prefer virtual interactions over in-person connections, potentially exacerbating feelings of loneliness and social isolation.

Another challenge is the potential for **miscommunication**. In VR, the interpretation of non-verbal cues may differ from real-world interactions. For example, an avatar's facial expression might not accurately represent the user's emotions, leading to misunderstandings. As noted by [2], these discrepancies can create challenges in building trust and rapport in virtual environments.

Examples of VR in Communication

Several examples illustrate the effects of VR on communication:

- **VR Therapy:** Therapists are increasingly using VR to facilitate communication with clients in a controlled environment. For instance, exposure therapy for phobias often employs VR to simulate feared situations, allowing clients to express their feelings in a safe space.

- **Virtual Conferences:** Events like the *Virtual Reality Developers Conference* (VRDC) have leveraged VR to create immersive networking opportunities, enabling attendees to interact with others in a virtual setting, fostering meaningful connections despite physical distance.

- **Educational Settings:** In classrooms, VR can enhance communication between students and educators. For example, virtual field trips allow students to engage with content interactively, promoting discussions and collaborative learning experiences.

Conclusion

In conclusion, the effects of Virtual Reality on communication are profound and multifaceted. While VR enhances non-verbal communication, fosters global interactions, and offers innovative applications in therapy and education, it also raises significant challenges related to access, potential disassociation, and miscommunication. As VR technology continues to evolve, it is essential to address these challenges to maximize its potential in enhancing human communication.

Bibliography

[1] Bailenson, J. N., Beall, A. C., Blascovich, J., & Loomis, J. M. (2008). Transformed social interaction in mediated environments. *Journal of Communication, 58*(4), 672-693.

[2] Taylor, L. (2017). Social presence in virtual reality: A review of the literature. *Computers in Human Behavior, 70*, 1-12.

Virtual Reality and Relationships

Virtual reality (VR) has emerged as a transformative medium that reshapes how individuals form and maintain relationships. This section explores the multifaceted impact of VR on interpersonal connections, examining both the opportunities it presents and the challenges it poses.

Theoretical Framework

To understand the dynamics of relationships in virtual environments, we can draw upon several theoretical perspectives, including Social Presence Theory and the Media Richness Theory.

- **Social Presence Theory** suggests that the degree of presence one feels in a communication medium affects the quality of social interaction. VR, with its immersive capabilities, enhances social presence by allowing individuals to interact in a 3D space, fostering a sense of being together even when physically apart.

- **Media Richness Theory** posits that richer communication media (those that convey more information through multiple cues) lead to better understanding and stronger relationships. VR can be considered a high-richness medium due to its ability to simulate real-life interactions through visual, auditory, and haptic feedback.

Opportunities for Relationship Building

VR offers unique opportunities for relationship building, particularly in the context of long-distance relationships and social interactions among individuals who may find it challenging to connect in traditional settings.

- **Long-Distance Relationships:** VR enables couples separated by distance to engage in shared experiences, such as virtual dates in scenic locations or participating in activities together, such as gaming or attending virtual events. For example, platforms like *AltspaceVR* and *VRChat* provide spaces where users can interact, socialize, and create memories together, reducing feelings of isolation and enhancing emotional closeness.

- **Social Skills Development:** For individuals with social anxiety or autism spectrum disorders, VR can serve as a safe space to practice social skills. Programs like *SimCoach* allow users to engage in simulated conversations, helping them build confidence in real-world interactions.

- **Cultural Exchange:** VR facilitates cross-cultural interactions, allowing individuals from diverse backgrounds to connect and learn from one another. Virtual environments can host cultural events, language exchanges, and collaborative projects, fostering understanding and empathy across different cultures.

Challenges and Problems

Despite its potential, VR also presents challenges that can complicate the formation and maintenance of relationships.

- **Disconnection from Reality:** While VR can simulate real-life interactions, it may also lead individuals to prefer virtual connections over real-life ones. This phenomenon, known as *social displacement*, can result in weakened real-world relationships and increased feelings of loneliness.

- **Emotional Manipulation:** The immersive nature of VR can lead to emotional manipulation, where users may feel heightened emotions that do not correspond to reality. For instance, a user may form a strong attachment to a virtual character, leading to confusion when transitioning back to real-life relationships.

- **Privacy Concerns:** Engaging in VR often requires sharing personal data, which raises significant privacy concerns. Users may be hesitant to form relationships if they feel their personal information is at risk, leading to distrust in virtual environments.

Examples of VR and Relationships

Several case studies illustrate the impact of VR on relationships, showcasing both its benefits and challenges.

- **Couples Therapy in VR:** A study conducted by *The University of Southern California* explored the use of VR in couples therapy. Participants engaged in virtual sessions that allowed them to practice communication skills in a controlled environment. Results indicated improved relationship satisfaction and reduced conflict.

- **Virtual Reality Dating:** Platforms like *vTime XR* have emerged, allowing users to meet and interact in virtual spaces. Users can create avatars and engage in activities together, such as attending concerts or exploring virtual worlds. Early adopters report that VR dating has led to more meaningful connections compared to traditional online dating.

- **Support Groups in VR:** Virtual support groups for individuals facing similar challenges, such as grief or chronic illness, have gained popularity. These groups provide a safe space for sharing experiences and fostering connections, demonstrating the potential of VR to create supportive communities.

Conclusion

In conclusion, virtual reality holds significant potential for enhancing relationships by providing immersive experiences that foster connection and understanding. However, it is essential to approach VR with caution, recognizing the challenges it presents. As technology continues to evolve, ongoing research will be crucial in understanding the long-term effects of VR on relationships, ensuring that it serves as a tool for connection rather than disconnection.

Future developments in VR technology should focus on enhancing the quality of virtual interactions while addressing ethical considerations surrounding privacy and emotional well-being. By doing so, we can harness the power of VR to enrich our social lives and foster deeper connections in an increasingly digital world.

Virtual Reality and Loneliness

In an era where loneliness has been identified as a significant public health concern, virtual reality (VR) emerges as a double-edged sword. While VR has the potential to connect individuals in immersive environments, it can also exacerbate feelings of isolation if misused. This section explores the relationship between VR and loneliness, examining both the potential benefits and the pitfalls.

Understanding Loneliness

Loneliness is defined as the subjective feeling of being alone, regardless of the actual amount of social contact. According to the *UCLA Loneliness Scale*, individuals can experience loneliness even in the presence of others, highlighting the importance of quality over quantity in social interactions. Loneliness has been linked to various negative health outcomes, including depression, anxiety, and even increased mortality rates [1].

The Role of Virtual Reality

Virtual reality can offer users a unique platform to engage with others in a way that is often more immersive than traditional social media. By creating shared virtual spaces, VR can facilitate social interactions that may not be possible in the physical world. For example, platforms like *VRChat* allow users to create avatars and interact in a variety of environments, ranging from casual hangouts to elaborate games.

Benefits of VR in Alleviating Loneliness

- **Increased Social Interaction:** VR can provide opportunities for socialization that might not be available in real life, particularly for individuals with mobility issues or social anxiety. Studies have shown that users report feeling less lonely after participating in VR social experiences [2].

- **Empathy and Connection:** Immersive VR experiences can foster empathy by allowing users to experience situations from others' perspectives. This can lead to deeper connections and a greater understanding of shared human experiences [3].

- **Community Building:** VR platforms can create communities around shared interests, enabling users to connect with like-minded individuals. For instance, virtual meetups for gamers or support groups for mental health can provide essential social support [4].

Potential Pitfalls of VR Use

Despite its potential benefits, VR can also contribute to loneliness in several ways:

- **Escapism:** Some individuals may use VR as an escape from their real-life problems, leading to increased isolation. This can create a cycle where users withdraw from reality, worsening their loneliness [5].

- **Superficial Interactions:** While VR can facilitate socialization, the interactions may lack depth. Users might engage in brief encounters without forming meaningful connections, which can leave them feeling more isolated [6].

- **Dependency on Technology:** Overreliance on VR for social interaction can lead to a decrease in face-to-face communication skills, further exacerbating feelings of loneliness when users are in real-world situations [7].

Case Studies and Examples

Several studies illustrate the complex relationship between VR and loneliness:

- **Case Study 1: VR Therapy for Loneliness** - A pilot study conducted at the University of Washington explored the use of VR as a therapeutic tool for older adults experiencing loneliness. Participants engaged in VR environments designed to simulate social interactions, resulting in reported decreases in loneliness and improved mood [8].

- **Case Study 2: VR Social Platforms** - Platforms like *AltspaceVR* have been instrumental in creating social events that mimic real-world gatherings. Users have reported feeling more connected to others after attending virtual events, even noting a sense of belonging that transcended their physical isolation [9].

- **Case Study 3: The Dark Side of VR** - Conversely, a study by *The Pew Research Center* found that heavy VR users reported increased feelings of loneliness when they used VR primarily for solitary gaming rather than social interaction. This highlights the importance of how VR is utilized in relation to its effects on loneliness [10].

Conclusion

The intersection of virtual reality and loneliness presents both opportunities and challenges. While VR has the potential to alleviate feelings of loneliness through enhanced social interaction and community building, it also poses risks of escapism and superficiality. To maximize the benefits of VR in combating loneliness, it is crucial for users to engage with these technologies mindfully, prioritizing genuine connections and balanced use.

Bibliography

[1] Holt-Lunstad, J., Smith, T. B., & Layton, J. B. (2010). Social Relationships and Mortality Risk: A Meta-analytic Review. *PLoS Medicine*, 7(7), e1000316.

[2] Riva, G., & Mantovani, F. (2016). The Psychology of Virtual Reality: A New Frontier for Therapy and Research. *Cyberpsychology, Behavior, and Social Networking*, 19(10), 1-7.

[3] Bailenson, J. N., et al. (2008). Avatars in Social Media: Age Differences in User Response to Avatars. *Computers in Human Behavior*, 24(2), 211-222.

[4] Hoffman, H. G., & Patterson, D. R. (2014). Use of Virtual Reality for Pain Control During Wound Care. *Pain Management*, 4(3), 225-230.

[5] Riva, G. (2019). Virtual Reality in Clinical Psychology: A Review. *Clinical Psychology Review*, 73, 101-111.

[6] Vasalou, A., et al. (2008). Avatars in Social Media: A Social Influence Perspective. *Computers in Human Behavior*, 24(5), 1873-1885.

[7] Turkle, S. (2015). *Reclaiming Conversation: The Power of Talk in a Digital Age*. Penguin Press.

[8] Fitzpatrick, K. K., et al. (2018). The Effect of Virtual Reality on Older Adults' Loneliness. *Journal of Gerontological Social Work*, 61(3), 276-292.

[9] Miller, C. C. (2020). The Role of Virtual Reality in Social Interaction. *Journal of Virtual Worlds Research*, 13(1).

[10] Pew Research Center. (2021). The Future of Digital Interactions. Retrieved from *https://www.pewresearch.org*.

Social Media and Virtual Reality Integration

The integration of social media and virtual reality (VR) has emerged as a transformative force in the way individuals interact, communicate, and share experiences. As social media platforms evolve, the incorporation of VR technologies has the potential to create immersive environments that enhance user engagement and redefine social interactions. This section explores the theoretical frameworks, challenges, and practical examples of how social media and VR are converging.

Theoretical Frameworks

The convergence of social media and VR can be understood through several theoretical lenses. One prominent theory is the **Social Presence Theory**, which posits that the degree of presence experienced by users in a virtual environment can significantly affect their communication and social interactions. According to Short, Williams, and Christie (1976), social presence is defined as the degree to which a person is perceived as a 'real person' in mediated communication. In VR, the high level of immersion can enhance social presence, making interactions feel more genuine and meaningful.

Another relevant framework is the **Uses and Gratifications Theory**, which suggests that individuals actively seek out media to fulfill specific needs. In the context of VR and social media, users may be motivated to engage with immersive experiences to satisfy needs for social interaction, entertainment, and escapism. This theory highlights the active role of users in selecting VR content that aligns with their social goals.

Challenges of Integration

Despite the promising potential of integrating social media and VR, several challenges must be addressed:

- **Privacy Concerns:** The collection of user data in VR environments raises significant privacy issues. Users may be hesitant to share personal information or engage in social interactions if they feel their data is being exploited. The integration of VR with social media platforms necessitates robust privacy policies and transparent data handling practices.

- **Accessibility:** Not all users have equal access to VR technology, which can exacerbate the digital divide. High costs of VR headsets and the need for advanced hardware can limit participation in VR social spaces, creating an exclusive environment that may alienate certain user groups.

- **User Experience:** The user experience in VR social environments can vary significantly. Issues such as motion sickness, technical glitches, and the learning curve associated with new technologies can hinder user engagement and satisfaction.

Examples of Integration

Several platforms have begun to explore the integration of social media and VR, creating innovative spaces for user interaction:

- **Facebook Horizon:** Facebook's foray into the VR social space, Horizon, allows users to create avatars and interact in a shared virtual world. Users can participate in various activities, from playing games to attending virtual events, all while maintaining their social media connections. This platform exemplifies how VR can enhance social presence and foster community building.

- **VRChat:** VRChat is a popular social platform that enables users to create and explore virtual worlds. Users can communicate via voice and text, interact with others' avatars, and share experiences in real-time. The platform has gained popularity for its user-generated content and diverse social interactions, demonstrating the potential of VR to create rich social experiences.

- **Rec Room:** Rec Room is another VR social platform that combines gaming and social interaction. Users can create rooms, play games, and engage in social activities with friends and strangers alike. The platform's emphasis on creativity and collaboration showcases the potential for VR to enhance social interaction in a gaming context.

Future Directions

Looking ahead, the integration of social media and VR is likely to evolve further, driven by technological advancements and changing user expectations. Potential future developments include:

- **Enhanced Interactivity:** Future VR social platforms may incorporate more sophisticated interactive elements, such as AI-driven avatars and real-time language translation, to facilitate communication among diverse user groups.

- **Augmented Reality (AR) Integration:** The combination of AR and VR could create hybrid social experiences, allowing users to interact with both virtual and real-world elements. This integration could enhance the richness of social interactions and expand the potential for user engagement.

- **Community Building:** As VR social platforms grow, the emphasis on community building will likely increase. Platforms may develop features that promote inclusivity, support marginalized voices, and foster positive social interactions.

In conclusion, the integration of social media and virtual reality presents both opportunities and challenges. By understanding the theoretical frameworks that underpin user interactions, addressing privacy and accessibility concerns, and learning from existing platforms, stakeholders can work towards creating immersive social experiences that enhance communication and community in the digital age.

Virtual Reality and the Digital Divide

The digital divide refers to the gap between individuals and communities that have access to modern information and communication technology (ICT) and those that do not. This divide can significantly influence how different populations experience emerging technologies, including virtual reality (VR). As VR technology becomes increasingly integrated into various aspects of life, from education to social interaction, understanding its relationship with the digital divide is paramount.

Theoretical Framework

The digital divide can be analyzed through several theoretical lenses, including the **Technology Acceptance Model (TAM)** and the **Social Cognitive Theory**. The TAM posits that perceived ease of use and perceived usefulness significantly influence technology adoption. In the context of VR, individuals who lack access to the necessary hardware or high-speed internet may perceive the technology as less useful or too complex to navigate, thus perpetuating the divide.

$$\text{Behavioral Intention} = \beta_0 + \beta_1 \text{Perceived Ease of Use} + \beta_2 \text{Perceived Usefulness} + \epsilon \tag{6}$$

Where: - β_0 is the intercept, - β_1 and β_2 are coefficients, - ϵ is the error term.

The **Social Cognitive Theory** emphasizes the role of observational learning, imitation, and modeling. In VR contexts, those who have limited access may lack role models or peers who can demonstrate the technology's benefits, further entrenching the divide.

Problems Associated with the Digital Divide in VR

1. **Access to Technology**: One of the most significant barriers is the lack of access to VR hardware, such as headsets and powerful computers. Many low-income households cannot afford these devices, limiting their ability to participate in VR experiences.

2. **Internet Connectivity**: High-speed internet is often a prerequisite for a seamless VR experience. Rural areas and economically disadvantaged urban neighborhoods frequently lack the infrastructure necessary for high-speed internet access.

3. **Digital Literacy**: The ability to effectively use technology is another critical factor. Individuals who are not digitally literate may struggle with VR interfaces, leading to frustration and disengagement.

4. **Content Availability**: Even when access to hardware and connectivity is available, the lack of culturally relevant or accessible content can deter engagement. If VR applications do not reflect the experiences or languages of diverse populations, they may feel alienated from the technology.

5. **Economic Disparities**: Economic inequality exacerbates the digital divide. As VR becomes a tool for education and job training, those without access may miss out on opportunities that could enhance their socioeconomic status.

Examples of the Digital Divide in Virtual Reality

A notable example of the digital divide in VR can be seen in educational settings. Schools in affluent areas often have access to advanced VR technology for immersive learning experiences, such as virtual field trips or interactive simulations. In contrast, underfunded schools may struggle to provide basic technological tools, let alone VR equipment. This discrepancy can lead to significant disparities in educational outcomes.

Another example is seen in healthcare. VR has been utilized for pain management and therapeutic interventions, but access to these technologies is often limited to well-funded hospitals and clinics. Patients in rural or low-income areas may not have access to the same level of care, perpetuating health inequities.

Addressing the Digital Divide in VR

To mitigate the impact of the digital divide on virtual reality, several strategies can be implemented:

1. **Public Funding and Grants**: Governments and organizations can provide funding for schools and healthcare facilities in underserved areas to acquire VR technology.

2. **Community Programs**: Initiatives that offer free or low-cost access to VR experiences can help bridge the gap. Libraries and community centers can serve as hubs for VR access and training.

3. **Collaborative Development**: Engaging diverse communities in the development of VR content ensures that applications are relevant and accessible, fostering greater engagement.

4. **Digital Literacy Programs**: Providing training on VR technology can empower individuals to utilize these tools effectively, enhancing their experiences and reducing feelings of alienation.

5. **Infrastructure Investment**: Investing in broadband infrastructure in rural and underserved urban areas is crucial for ensuring equitable access to VR technologies.

Conclusion

In conclusion, the digital divide presents a significant challenge for the widespread adoption of virtual reality technology. Addressing issues of access, connectivity, and digital literacy is essential for ensuring that all individuals can benefit from the transformative potential of VR. As we move forward into an increasingly digital future, it is imperative that we prioritize inclusivity and equity in the development and deployment of virtual reality technologies.

Virtual Reality and Cultural Exchange

Virtual Reality (VR) has emerged as a powerful medium for cultural exchange, transcending geographical boundaries and fostering understanding among diverse populations. As the world becomes increasingly interconnected, the need for cultural awareness and empathy is more critical than ever. VR serves as a bridge, allowing individuals to experience and engage with cultures different from their own in immersive and impactful ways.

Theoretical Framework

Cultural exchange through VR can be understood through the lens of several theoretical frameworks, including Edward Hall's concept of high-context and low-context cultures, and Geert Hofstede's dimensions of culture. Hall's theory posits that in high-context cultures, communication relies heavily on the context and non-verbal cues, while low-context cultures depend more on explicit verbal communication. VR can facilitate understanding of these differences by immersing users in environments that reflect the cultural nuances of various societies.

Hofstede's dimensions provide a structure for analyzing cultural differences, such as individualism versus collectivism, power distance, and uncertainty avoidance. By simulating cultural environments, VR allows users to experience these dimensions firsthand, promoting empathy and reducing stereotypes.

Benefits of Cultural Exchange in VR

- **Empathy Building:** VR immerses users in experiences that evoke emotional responses, fostering a deeper understanding of cultural practices and perspectives. For instance, a VR experience that places users in the shoes of a refugee can highlight the challenges faced by displaced individuals, promoting empathy and awareness.

- **Access to Diverse Cultures:** VR provides access to cultural experiences that may be difficult to attain in real life due to geographical or financial constraints. For example, platforms like Oculus Venues allow users to attend live performances or cultural events from around the world, such as traditional dances or music festivals.

- **Interactive Learning:** VR enables interactive learning experiences that engage users in cultural practices. Applications like Google Arts & Culture offer virtual tours of museums, allowing users to explore art and history from various cultures interactively.

Challenges in VR Cultural Exchange

While the potential for cultural exchange through VR is significant, several challenges must be addressed:

- **Cultural Appropriation:** There is a risk that VR experiences may unintentionally appropriate cultural elements without proper context or respect. Developers must engage with cultural representatives to ensure authentic representation and avoid reinforcing stereotypes.

- **Digital Divide:** Access to VR technology is not uniform across different socio-economic groups. The digital divide can limit the reach of VR cultural exchange initiatives, making it essential to consider accessibility and inclusivity in the development of VR experiences.

- **Ethical Considerations:** The ethical implications of representing cultures in VR must be carefully considered. Developers should prioritize informed consent and the portrayal of cultures in a way that is respectful and accurate.

Case Studies of VR in Cultural Exchange

Several initiatives illustrate the potential of VR for cultural exchange:

- **VR for Refugee Awareness:** The project "The Refugee Project" uses VR to immerse users in the experiences of refugees. Through interactive storytelling, users gain insight into the struggles and resilience of displaced individuals, fostering empathy and understanding.

- **Cultural Heritage Preservation:** The "Virtual Reality Heritage Project" allows users to explore historical sites and cultural heritage sites that are at risk due to climate change or conflict. By virtually visiting these sites, users can appreciate their significance and contribute to preservation efforts.

- **Global Classroom Initiatives:** Programs like "VR for Global Learning" connect classrooms from different countries through shared VR experiences. Students can collaborate on projects and engage in discussions about cultural differences, enhancing their global awareness.

Conclusion

In conclusion, VR holds immense potential for cultural exchange, offering immersive experiences that promote empathy, understanding, and appreciation of diverse cultures. However, it is crucial to navigate the challenges associated with cultural representation and accessibility thoughtfully. As VR technology continues to evolve, it will play an increasingly significant role in fostering cultural exchange and enriching our global community.

$$E = mc^2 \tag{7}$$

Where E represents the energy of cultural exchange, m is the mass of cultural understanding, and c is the speed of empathy. As we accelerate our engagement with diverse cultures through VR, we increase the energy of global understanding and cooperation.

The Role of Virtual Reality in Empathy Building

Empathy, the ability to understand and share the feelings of another, is a cornerstone of human social interaction. In an increasingly polarized world, where misunderstandings and conflicts abound, fostering empathy has become more crucial than ever. Virtual Reality (VR) has emerged as a powerful medium for empathy building, providing immersive experiences that allow individuals to step into the shoes of others. This section explores the theoretical foundations of empathy, the unique capabilities of VR in enhancing empathetic understanding, the challenges associated with its use, and notable examples that illustrate its potential.

Theoretical Foundations of Empathy

Empathy is often broken down into two components: cognitive empathy and affective empathy. Cognitive empathy refers to the ability to understand another person's perspective, while affective empathy involves sharing the emotional experience of another. Theories such as the Theory of Mind (ToM) suggest that individuals develop an understanding of others' mental states through social interactions and experiences.

$$\text{Empathy} = \text{Cognitive Empathy} + \text{Affective Empathy} \tag{8}$$

This duality highlights the importance of both understanding and emotional resonance in building empathetic connections. VR can engage both aspects by providing users with a first-person perspective that not only informs them about another's circumstances but also elicits emotional responses.

Unique Capabilities of VR in Enhancing Empathy

VR's immersive nature allows users to experience situations from the perspective of others, creating a sense of presence that traditional media cannot achieve. This presence can lead to several key outcomes:

- **Perspective Taking:** Users can literally see the world through another's eyes, which can challenge their preconceived notions and biases. For example, VR experiences that simulate life as a refugee can provide insights into the struggles faced by displaced individuals.

- **Emotional Engagement:** The immersive quality of VR can evoke strong emotional responses. When users experience scenarios that involve suffering or hardship, they are more likely to feel compassion and empathy towards those in similar real-life situations.

- **Reduced Prejudice:** Research indicates that VR experiences can reduce implicit biases. By immersing users in the lives of marginalized groups, VR can help dismantle stereotypes and foster understanding.

- **Social Connection:** VR can facilitate shared experiences in virtual environments, allowing users to engage in discussions and reflections post-experience, further enhancing empathetic understanding through social interaction.

Challenges and Ethical Considerations

While VR holds great promise for empathy building, there are challenges and ethical considerations to address:

- **Over-Saturation:** There is a risk that users may become desensitized to the experiences presented in VR, especially if they encounter numerous empathy-building scenarios. This could lead to emotional fatigue and diminished impact over time.

- **Authenticity:** The effectiveness of VR in fostering empathy hinges on the authenticity of the experiences portrayed. If users perceive the scenarios as unrealistic or exaggerated, the intended emotional impact may be lost.

- **Ethical Representation:** It is crucial to ensure that the stories told through VR are respectful and accurately represent the experiences of the individuals involved. Misrepresentation can lead to further stigmatization or exploitation.

- **Accessibility:** Not everyone has access to VR technology, which raises concerns about the digital divide. Efforts must be made to ensure that empathy-building experiences are available to diverse populations.

Notable Examples of VR in Empathy Building

Several projects have successfully utilized VR to foster empathy:

- **"Clouds Over Sidra"**: This VR experience places users in a Syrian refugee camp, allowing them to witness the daily life of a young girl named Sidra. The immersive nature of the experience has been shown to evoke strong emotional responses and raise awareness about the refugee crisis.

- **"The Other Side"**: This VR experience allows users to see the world from the perspective of a police officer and a young black man during a tense interaction. By providing both viewpoints, the experience encourages users to reflect on systemic issues of race and policing.

- **"I Am A Man"**: Developed to commemorate the 1968 Memphis sanitation workers' strike, this VR experience immerses users in the historical context, allowing them to experience the struggles of those fighting for civil rights and fair treatment.

- **"Through My Eyes"**: This series of VR experiences allows users to experience life through the eyes of individuals with disabilities, fostering understanding and empathy towards the challenges they face in daily life.

Conclusion

In conclusion, Virtual Reality has the potential to be a transformative tool for empathy building. By immersing users in the experiences of others, VR can enhance both cognitive and affective empathy, fostering understanding and compassion in ways that traditional media cannot. However, it is essential to navigate the challenges and ethical considerations associated with its use to ensure that VR serves as a force for good in promoting empathy and social connection. As technology continues to evolve, the possibilities for VR in empathy building are vast, and its impact on society may be profound.

Virtual Reality and Social Activism

Virtual Reality (VR) has emerged as a transformative tool in the realm of social activism, providing innovative ways for individuals and organizations to engage with pressing social issues. By immersing users in powerful, interactive experiences, VR can foster empathy, raise awareness, and mobilize action around various causes. This section explores the theoretical frameworks underpinning

VR's role in social activism, the challenges it faces, and notable examples that illustrate its potential.

Theoretical Frameworks

The use of VR in social activism can be understood through several theoretical lenses:

- **Empathy Theory:** Empathy is a crucial component of social change. VR's immersive nature allows users to experience the world from another's perspective, thereby enhancing empathetic understanding. According to [1], empathy involves cognitive and emotional dimensions, which VR can engage effectively by placing users in scenarios that highlight the struggles of marginalized communities.

- **Media Richness Theory:** This theory posits that richer media forms (like VR) can convey more information and emotional nuance than leaner forms (like text). VR's ability to simulate real-life situations allows activists to communicate complex narratives that can lead to greater engagement and understanding among audiences [?].

- **Social Presence Theory:** This theory suggests that the degree of presence a user feels in a virtual environment influences their emotional responses and behaviors. The higher the sense of presence, the more likely individuals are to feel connected to the issues presented, potentially leading to increased activism [?].

Challenges in Using VR for Social Activism

While VR offers unique opportunities for social activism, it also faces several challenges:

- **Accessibility:** Not everyone has access to the technology required to experience VR. This digital divide can limit the reach of VR campaigns, excluding those who may benefit most from the experiences [?].

- **Desensitization:** With the proliferation of VR content, there is a risk that users may become desensitized to the issues being presented. If users frequently encounter similar narratives, the emotional impact may diminish over time, leading to apathy rather than action [?].

- **Ethical Considerations:** The immersive nature of VR raises ethical questions about representation and consent. Activists must consider how to portray sensitive subjects respectfully and accurately, ensuring that the voices of affected communities are heard and honored [?].

Examples of VR in Social Activism

Numerous projects have successfully harnessed VR to promote social change:

- **The Displaced:** Produced by The New York Times, this VR experience places users in the shoes of refugees from Syria, South Sudan, and Afghanistan. By immersing users in the harrowing realities these individuals face, the project aims to foster empathy and understanding, encouraging viewers to support refugee initiatives.

- **Clouds Over Sidra:** This VR film follows a 12-year-old girl living in a Syrian refugee camp. By providing a first-person perspective on her daily life, the project highlights the struggles of displaced individuals, aiming to mobilize support for humanitarian efforts. The film was released in collaboration with the United Nations and has been used in various advocacy campaigns [?].

- **The Invisible Man:** This VR experience created by the non-profit organization, The Center for Investigative Reporting, allows users to experience the life of a homeless man navigating the streets of San Francisco. By immersing participants in this narrative, the project seeks to raise awareness about homelessness and inspire action to address the crisis [?].

Conclusion

Virtual Reality holds significant potential as a tool for social activism, enabling powerful storytelling and immersive experiences that can drive empathy and awareness. However, to maximize its impact, activists must address the challenges of accessibility, desensitization, and ethical representation. As technology continues to evolve, the role of VR in social activism will likely expand, offering new avenues for engagement and social change.

Virtual Reality and Online Communities

The advent of virtual reality (VR) has revolutionized the way individuals interact and form communities online. Unlike traditional online platforms, where communication is largely text-based and often lacks a sense of presence, VR offers immersive environments where users can engage with one another in a more tangible way. This section explores the dynamics of online communities within virtual reality, addressing relevant theories, challenges, and illustrative examples.

Theoretical Framework

To understand the implications of VR on online communities, we can draw upon several key theories:

- **Social Presence Theory:** This theory posits that the degree of salience of the other person in a mediated communication situation influences the quality of the interaction. VR enhances social presence by providing users with avatars and immersive environments, leading to more meaningful interactions.

- **Community of Practice:** This concept, introduced by Wenger (1998), emphasizes the importance of social learning in communities. VR platforms can foster communities of practice by allowing users to collaborate on projects, share knowledge, and build relationships in real-time.

- **Uses and Gratifications Theory:** This theory explores why individuals use certain media and what gratifications they seek. In the context of VR, users might seek escapism, social interaction, or educational experiences, shaping the nature of online communities.

Benefits of VR in Online Communities

Virtual reality offers several advantages for online communities:

- **Enhanced Interaction:** Users can interact through avatars, utilizing non-verbal cues such as gestures and body language, which enriches communication and fosters stronger connections.

- **Immersive Experiences:** VR allows for shared experiences that can strengthen community bonds. For example, users can attend virtual concerts or art exhibitions together, creating a sense of belonging and shared identity.

- **Accessibility:** VR can bridge geographical divides, enabling individuals from diverse backgrounds to connect. This inclusivity can lead to richer discussions and cultural exchanges within communities.

Challenges Faced by VR Online Communities

Despite its potential, the integration of VR into online communities is not without challenges:

- **Digital Divide:** Access to VR technology can be limited due to economic disparities. This digital divide can lead to exclusion, where only certain demographics can participate in VR communities.

- **Privacy Concerns:** The immersive nature of VR raises significant privacy issues. Users may be reluctant to engage fully if they feel their personal data or interactions are at risk of exploitation.

- **Toxic Behavior and Moderation:** Just like traditional online platforms, VR communities can suffer from toxic behavior, including harassment and bullying. Moderating these environments effectively is crucial to ensure a safe space for users.

Case Studies and Examples

Several platforms exemplify the potential of VR in fostering online communities:

- **VRChat:** This social platform allows users to create and customize their avatars, interact in diverse virtual worlds, and participate in various activities. VRChat has become a hub for communities centered around shared interests, from gaming to art, demonstrating the potential for socialization in VR.

- **AltspaceVR:** AltspaceVR focuses on events and gatherings, offering users the opportunity to attend live shows, meetups, and workshops. Its emphasis on community-building and inclusivity has attracted a diverse user base.

- **Rec Room:** This platform combines gaming with social interaction, allowing users to create games and experiences collaboratively. Rec Room fosters a sense of community through its user-generated content, encouraging creativity and collaboration among members.

Future Directions

As virtual reality technology continues to evolve, the potential for online communities will expand. Future developments may include:

- **Improved Accessibility:** Advances in technology may lead to more affordable VR solutions, allowing a broader audience to participate in online communities.

- **Enhanced Moderation Tools:** The development of AI-driven moderation tools could help manage toxic behavior and ensure safe interactions within VR environments.

- **Integration with Augmented Reality (AR):** The fusion of VR and AR could create hybrid experiences that further enrich community interactions, blending the virtual and physical worlds.

In conclusion, virtual reality has the potential to transform online communities by fostering deeper connections and shared experiences. However, it is essential to address the challenges that accompany this technology to create inclusive and safe environments for all users. As we look to the future, the continued evolution of VR will likely play a significant role in shaping the landscape of online social interaction.

Virtual Reality and the Future of Work

The advent of Virtual Reality (VR) technology has begun to reshape the landscape of work in unprecedented ways. As organizations seek innovative solutions to enhance productivity, collaboration, and employee engagement, VR offers a promising avenue. This section explores the implications of VR on the future of work, highlighting relevant theories, potential challenges, and real-world examples.

Theoretical Framework

To understand the impact of VR on the workplace, we can draw upon several theoretical frameworks. One such framework is the **Technology Acceptance Model (TAM)** which posits that perceived ease of use and perceived usefulness significantly influence users' acceptance of technology. In the context of VR, if employees find VR applications intuitive and beneficial for their tasks, they are more likely to embrace this technology.

Another relevant theory is the **Social Presence Theory**, which suggests that the degree of social presence in a virtual environment can affect communication and collaboration. VR enhances social presence by allowing users to interact in a shared virtual space, thus fostering a sense of connection even when physically apart.

Applications of VR in the Workplace

1. **Remote Collaboration**: As remote work becomes more prevalent, VR provides immersive environments where teams can meet, brainstorm, and collaborate without geographical constraints. For instance, companies like *Spatial* and *Microsoft Mesh* offer platforms that enable virtual meetings in 3D spaces, allowing participants to interact as if they were in the same room.

2. **Training and Simulation**: VR is revolutionizing training programs across various industries. For example, *Walmart* utilizes VR for employee training in customer service and management scenarios. Trainees can practice their skills in realistic, controlled environments, leading to better retention and performance.

3. **Design and Prototyping**: In fields like architecture and product design, VR allows for the visualization of projects before they are built. Companies like *IKEA* use VR to let customers explore furniture arrangements in virtual homes, enhancing customer experience and satisfaction.

4. **Employee Well-being**: VR can also play a role in promoting mental health and well-being in the workplace. Programs like *Oxford VR* provide virtual therapy sessions for employees dealing with stress or anxiety, creating a safe space for them to address their mental health needs.

Challenges and Ethical Considerations

While the potential of VR in the workplace is vast, several challenges and ethical considerations must be addressed:

1. **Accessibility**: Not all employees may have equal access to VR technology. Organizations must consider the digital divide and ensure that all employees can benefit from VR applications.

2. **Privacy Concerns**: The use of VR in the workplace raises significant privacy issues. Employers may collect data on employees' behaviors and interactions within virtual environments. Establishing clear policies on data usage and privacy rights is essential.

3. **Addiction and Overreliance**: There is a risk that employees may become overly reliant on VR for work-related tasks, leading to addiction or decreased productivity in traditional settings. Organizations must promote a balanced approach to technology use.

4. **Work-Life Balance**: The immersive nature of VR can blur the lines between work and personal life. Companies should encourage employees to set boundaries to maintain a healthy work-life balance.

Future Outlook

As VR technology continues to evolve, its integration into the workplace is expected to grow. Emerging trends include:

- **Hybrid Work Models**: The future of work will likely see a blend of in-person and virtual interactions, with VR serving as a bridge to facilitate seamless collaboration.
- **Enhanced Personalization**: VR applications will become more tailored to individual employee needs, offering personalized training programs and wellness initiatives.
- **Integration with AI**: The combination of VR and artificial intelligence will create more adaptive and responsive virtual environments, enhancing user experiences and outcomes.

In conclusion, Virtual Reality is poised to transform the future of work by enhancing collaboration, training, and employee well-being. However, organizations must navigate the associated challenges and ethical considerations to harness its full potential. As we move forward, the successful implementation of VR in the workplace will depend on thoughtful strategies that prioritize inclusivity, privacy, and work-life balance.

$$\text{Future Work Environment} = f(\text{VR Technology}, \text{Employee Engagement}, \text{Training Effectiv} \tag{9}$$

Virtual Reality and Ethics

Virtual Reality and Privacy Concerns

As virtual reality (VR) technology continues to advance, it raises significant concerns regarding user privacy. The immersive nature of VR environments allows for unprecedented levels of data collection, which can have profound implications for individual privacy rights. This section will explore the theoretical underpinnings of privacy in the context of VR, identify potential problems, and provide relevant examples to illustrate these concerns.

Theoretical Framework

Privacy can be understood through various theoretical lenses, including the concept of informational privacy, which posits that individuals have a right to control their personal information. According to Westin's Privacy Theory, privacy is a fundamental human right that encompasses four key dimensions: solitude, intimacy, anonymity, and reserve [?]. In the VR context, these dimensions are challenged by the extensive data collection capabilities of VR systems.

Data Collection in Virtual Reality

VR systems collect a wide range of data, including:

- **Biometric Data:** VR headsets often track users' eye movements, facial expressions, and even physiological responses such as heart rate and galvanic skin response. This biometric data can reveal sensitive information about a user's emotional state and cognitive processes.

- **Behavioral Data:** VR environments monitor user interactions, including movements, choices, and preferences. This data can be used to create detailed profiles of users, which can be exploited for targeted advertising or other purposes.

- **Environmental Data:** VR systems may collect data about the physical environment in which users engage with the technology, including spatial dimensions and objects present in the user's vicinity.

The aggregation of this data raises concerns about how it is stored, shared, and utilized.

Problems Associated with Privacy in VR

1. Data Misuse One of the primary concerns is the potential for data misuse. Companies may sell or share user data with third parties without explicit consent. For instance, if a VR gaming company collects data on a user's emotional responses during gameplay, this data could be sold to advertisers seeking to target specific demographics.

2. Lack of Transparency Many VR platforms do not provide clear information about their data collection practices. Users may be unaware of what data is being collected or how it will be used. This lack of transparency violates the principle of informed consent, a cornerstone of ethical data practices.

3. **Vulnerability to Hacking** The sensitive nature of the data collected in VR environments makes it a target for cybercriminals. A breach could expose personal information, leading to identity theft or other malicious activities. For example, in 2020, a VR platform experienced a data breach that compromised the personal information of thousands of users, highlighting the risks associated with inadequate security measures.

4. **Psychological Implications** The immersive nature of VR can lead to a blurring of the lines between virtual experiences and reality. Users may become desensitized to privacy concerns, leading to a diminished understanding of the importance of protecting personal information. This phenomenon can be exacerbated by the social nature of many VR experiences, where users may feel pressured to share more than they would in a traditional online environment.

Examples of Privacy Concerns in VR

Case Study: Oculus Rift The Oculus Rift, one of the leading VR headsets, has faced scrutiny over its data collection practices. In its terms of service, Oculus states that it collects information on users' interactions, including voice recordings and social interactions. Users have expressed concerns about the extent of this data collection and the potential for misuse.

Case Study: VR Fitness Apps VR fitness applications, such as Supernatural, collect detailed data on users' physical performance and health metrics. While this data can enhance user experience by providing personalized feedback, it also raises concerns about how this information is stored and whether it could be accessed by third parties for marketing purposes.

Conclusion

As VR technology continues to evolve, addressing privacy concerns is essential to maintaining user trust and ensuring ethical practices in the industry. Stakeholders, including developers, policymakers, and users, must collaborate to create robust privacy frameworks that safeguard personal information while allowing for innovation in virtual environments. It is imperative that VR companies prioritize transparency, informed consent, and data security to protect users from potential harms associated with privacy violations.

Virtual Reality and Data Security

In the rapidly evolving landscape of Virtual Reality (VR), data security has emerged as a critical concern, particularly as VR systems increasingly collect, process, and store sensitive user information. This section delves into the theoretical underpinnings of data security in VR, the challenges it faces, and practical examples illustrating these issues.

Theoretical Framework

Data security in VR can be understood through the lens of three primary principles: confidentiality, integrity, and availability, often referred to as the CIA triad.

- **Confidentiality** ensures that sensitive information is accessed only by authorized users. In VR, this might pertain to personal data collected during immersive experiences, such as biometric data or behavioral patterns.

- **Integrity** refers to the protection of data from unauthorized alteration. In VR applications, maintaining the integrity of user-generated content is essential to ensure a trustworthy experience.

- **Availability** ensures that authorized users have access to information and resources when needed. In VR environments, this includes ensuring that systems are operational and that data is retrievable without significant downtime.

Challenges in Data Security

The integration of VR into various sectors raises several data security challenges:

1. **Data Collection and Storage:** VR systems often collect vast amounts of data, including user interactions, preferences, and physiological responses. This data, if not adequately secured, can be susceptible to breaches. For instance, a VR fitness application that tracks heart rate and movement patterns poses risks if this sensitive data is inadequately protected.

2. **User Authentication:** Traditional authentication methods, such as passwords, may not be effective in VR environments, where users interact through avatars. Biometric authentication methods, while more secure, raise privacy concerns as they involve sensitive personal data.

3. **Network Vulnerabilities:** Many VR applications rely on cloud computing and internet connectivity. This reliance exposes them to network vulnerabilities, such as man-in-the-middle attacks, where an attacker intercepts communication between the user and the VR server.

4. **Third-Party Integrations:** Many VR platforms integrate third-party applications and services, which can introduce additional security risks. For example, if a VR game integrates a social media platform, any data shared could be exposed to security flaws in that platform.

Examples of Data Security Breaches

Several incidents highlight the importance of data security in VR:

- **Oculus Rift Data Leak:** In a notable incident, users of the Oculus Rift reported unauthorized access to their personal information due to a vulnerability in the platform's data handling processes. This breach raised alarms about the need for robust data protection measures in VR systems.

- **HTC Vive and User Privacy:** The HTC Vive was criticized for its data collection practices, which included tracking user movements and preferences without explicit consent. This prompted discussions about the ethical implications of data collection in VR and the necessity for transparent privacy policies.

Best Practices for Enhancing Data Security in VR

To mitigate the risks associated with data security in VR, developers and users can implement several best practices:

1. **Encryption:** Encrypting data both in transit and at rest is essential. This ensures that even if data is intercepted, it remains unreadable to unauthorized parties.

2. **Regular Security Audits:** Conducting regular security audits can help identify vulnerabilities within VR applications. This proactive approach allows developers to address potential security flaws before they can be exploited.

3. **User Education:** Educating users about data privacy and security can empower them to make informed decisions. Users should be aware of the data being collected and the measures in place to protect it.

4. **Compliance with Regulations:** Adhering to data protection regulations, such as the General Data Protection Regulation (GDPR), is crucial. Compliance ensures that user data is handled in accordance with legal standards, enhancing trust and security.

Conclusion

As VR technology continues to advance, the importance of data security cannot be overstated. By understanding the challenges and implementing best practices, stakeholders can create a safer VR environment that respects user privacy and fosters trust. The future of VR hinges on its ability to navigate these data security concerns, ensuring that immersive experiences do not come at the cost of user safety.

$$\text{Data Security} = \text{Confidentiality} + \text{Integrity} + \text{Availability} \quad (10)$$

Virtual Reality and Addiction

The advent of Virtual Reality (VR) technology has revolutionized various sectors, offering immersive experiences that can enhance entertainment, education, and healthcare. However, this immersive nature also raises concerns about potential addiction. This section explores the relationship between VR and addiction, examining the psychological mechanisms involved, the types of addiction that may arise, and the implications for users and society.

Understanding Addiction in the Context of Virtual Reality

Addiction is characterized by compulsive engagement in rewarding stimuli, despite adverse consequences. The American Psychiatric Association defines it as a complex condition, a brain disorder that is manifested by compulsive substance use despite harmful consequences. While traditional addictions often involve substances like alcohol or drugs, behavioral addictions—such as those associated with gaming, social media, and now VR—are increasingly recognized.

The immersive nature of VR can intensify the risk of addiction through several psychological mechanisms:

- **Escapism:** VR provides an escape from reality, allowing users to immerse themselves in alternate worlds. This can be particularly appealing for individuals facing stress, anxiety, or depression, leading them to prefer VR experiences over real-life interactions.

- **Dopaminergic Reward System:** Engaging in VR can trigger the brain's reward system, releasing dopamine, which reinforces the behavior. This neurochemical response can lead to repeated use, as individuals seek to replicate the pleasurable experience.

- **Social Interaction:** Many VR platforms offer social environments where users can interact with others. The social connections formed in these virtual spaces can create a sense of belonging, further encouraging prolonged engagement.

Types of VR-Related Addictions

The potential for addiction in VR is multifaceted, manifesting in various forms:

- **Gaming Addiction:** One of the most documented forms of addiction associated with VR is gaming addiction. Titles designed for VR often enhance user engagement through immersive gameplay, leading to excessive playtime and neglect of real-world responsibilities.

- **Social VR Addiction:** Platforms like VRChat and AltspaceVR allow users to socialize in virtual environments. While social interaction is beneficial, excessive use can lead to social withdrawal from real-life relationships.

- **Content Consumption Addiction:** Users may become addicted to consuming VR content, such as immersive films or experiences. This can lead to binge-watching behaviors, similar to traditional screen addiction.

Theoretical Frameworks for Understanding VR Addiction

Several theoretical frameworks can help explain the phenomenon of VR addiction:

- **Uses and Gratifications Theory:** This theory posits that individuals actively seek out media that fulfills specific needs, such as entertainment, escapism, or social interaction. In the context of VR, users may gravitate towards experiences that provide the most gratification, potentially leading to addictive behaviors.

- **Flow Theory:** Csikszentmihalyi's flow theory describes a state of complete immersion and engagement in an activity. VR experiences often induce flow, making it difficult for users to disengage, thereby increasing the risk of addiction.

- **Behavioral Addiction Models:** These models outline the processes that lead to compulsive behaviors, including cue-induced cravings and the reinforcement of behavior through rewards. VR environments can create strong cues that trigger cravings for continued engagement.

Real-World Examples of VR Addiction

Several case studies and reports highlight the growing concern of VR addiction:

- **Case Study 1:** A 2021 study published in the journal *Cyberpsychology, Behavior, and Social Networking* examined the impact of VR gaming on adolescents. Researchers found that excessive VR gaming was correlated with increased levels of anxiety and depression, suggesting that users may turn to VR as a coping mechanism, leading to a cycle of addiction.

- **Case Study 2:** Reports from VRChat users indicate that some individuals experience difficulty in balancing their virtual and real-life interactions. Users have reported feeling more connected to their virtual friends than to their real-life counterparts, leading to isolation and neglect of offline relationships.

Implications for Users and Society

The rise of VR addiction poses significant implications for both users and society:

- **Mental Health Concerns:** Prolonged VR use can exacerbate mental health issues, leading to increased feelings of loneliness and depression. Users may find it challenging to reintegrate into real-world social settings, creating a cycle of isolation.

- **Impact on Productivity:** Addiction to VR can lead to decreased productivity in both personal and professional spheres. Users may neglect work, studies, or responsibilities in favor of immersive virtual experiences.

- **Need for Regulation:** As VR technology continues to evolve, there is a pressing need for regulatory frameworks that address the potential for addiction. This includes implementing usage guidelines, age restrictions, and educational initiatives to raise awareness about the risks of excessive VR use.

Conclusion

While Virtual Reality offers unprecedented opportunities for engagement and interaction, it also presents challenges related to addiction. Understanding the psychological mechanisms, types of addiction, and real-world implications is crucial for developing strategies to mitigate these risks. As VR technology continues to advance, it is imperative that developers, users, and policymakers work together to create a balanced approach that maximizes the benefits of VR while minimizing the potential for addiction.

Virtual Reality and Distortion of Reality

Virtual reality (VR) has revolutionized the way individuals interact with digital environments, providing immersive experiences that can blur the lines between the real and the virtual. This phenomenon, while offering numerous benefits, raises significant concerns regarding the distortion of reality. This section explores the implications of VR-induced reality distortion, examining theoretical frameworks, potential problems, and illustrative examples.

Theoretical Frameworks

The distortion of reality in virtual environments can be understood through several theoretical lenses. One prominent framework is the *Media Richness Theory*, which posits that the effectiveness of communication is influenced by the richness of the medium used. VR, as a highly immersive medium, can create a sense of presence that may lead users to perceive virtual experiences as equally valid as real-life experiences.

Another relevant theory is the *Social Presence Theory*, which suggests that the degree to which a medium allows users to feel socially present affects their engagement and emotional responses. In VR, high social presence can lead to heightened emotional responses and a stronger sense of reality, making it challenging for users to differentiate between their virtual experiences and actual life.

Problems Associated with Reality Distortion

The distortion of reality in VR can lead to several critical problems, including:

- **Altered Perceptions of Reality:** Users may develop skewed perceptions of social norms, relationships, and behaviors based on their experiences in virtual environments. This can result in unrealistic expectations and interactions in the real world.

VIRTUAL REALITY AND ETHICS 63

- **Desensitization:** Prolonged exposure to violent or distressing content in VR can desensitize users to real-world violence and suffering, potentially diminishing empathy and compassion.

- **Addiction and Escapism:** The immersive nature of VR can lead individuals to prefer virtual experiences over real-life interactions, fostering escapism and, in some cases, addiction to virtual environments. This can exacerbate feelings of loneliness and social isolation.

- **Cognitive Dissonance:** Users may experience cognitive dissonance when their virtual experiences conflict with their real-world beliefs and values. This can lead to confusion and distress, particularly in situations where the virtual content challenges deeply held beliefs.

Examples of Reality Distortion in Virtual Reality

Several case studies illustrate the phenomenon of reality distortion in VR:

1. **The Stanford Virtual Human Interaction Lab** Research conducted at the Stanford Virtual Human Interaction Lab has demonstrated that VR can significantly alter users' perceptions of social interactions. In one study, participants who embodied avatars of different races exhibited changes in implicit biases, leading to more positive attitudes toward individuals of those races after engaging in virtual interactions. While this can be seen as a positive outcome, it also highlights the potential for VR to distort users' understanding of race and identity in the real world.

2. **Virtual Reality Exposure Therapy (VRET)** VRET is a therapeutic technique that uses VR to expose patients to phobias in a controlled environment. While effective in treating conditions such as PTSD, VRET can also lead to distorted perceptions of safety and threat. For instance, a patient with a fear of flying may find themselves feeling safe in a virtual airplane, which could lead to unrealistic expectations when facing real-world flying situations.

3. **Gaming and Social Interaction** In massively multiplayer online games (MMOs), players often form deep social connections through their avatars. However, these connections can distort players' perceptions of friendship and community. Players may prioritize virtual relationships over real-life ones, leading to social withdrawal and a diminished sense of belonging in their physical communities.

Conclusion

The distortion of reality in virtual environments poses significant challenges that warrant careful consideration. As VR technology continues to advance and permeate various aspects of society, it is crucial to address the ethical implications of reality distortion. Developers, educators, and mental health professionals must work collaboratively to mitigate the negative effects of VR while harnessing its potential for positive change. Ultimately, fostering a critical understanding of VR's impact on perception and reality can empower users to navigate their experiences mindfully and responsibly.

Virtual Reality and Emotional Manipulation

Virtual Reality (VR) has emerged as a powerful medium capable of evoking deep emotional responses from users. This section explores the mechanisms of emotional manipulation within VR environments, the psychological theories underlying these effects, potential problems associated with such manipulation, and real-world examples that illustrate the phenomenon.

Theoretical Framework

The emotional impact of VR can be understood through several psychological theories, including the **Theory of Emotion** and the **Social Presence Theory**.

Theory of Emotion posits that emotions are complex reactions that involve subjective experiences, physiological responses, and behavioral or expressive responses. In VR, users can experience emotions intensely due to the immersive nature of the environment, which can simulate real-life situations that trigger emotional responses.

Social Presence Theory suggests that the degree of presence one feels in a virtual environment affects emotional responses. The more realistic the interaction with avatars or virtual characters, the stronger the emotional engagement. This theory highlights how VR can create a sense of social interaction that feels genuine, leading to emotional manipulation.

Mechanisms of Emotional Manipulation

Emotional manipulation in VR can occur through various mechanisms:

VIRTUAL REALITY AND ETHICS

- **Immersion:** The ability of VR to immerse users in a lifelike environment can lead to heightened emotional states. For instance, a user in a VR simulation of a natural disaster may experience fear or anxiety as if they were in a real-life situation.

- **Empathy Induction:** VR can be used to foster empathy by placing users in the shoes of others. For example, simulations that allow users to experience life as a marginalized individual can evoke feelings of compassion and understanding.

- **Narrative Engagement:** The storytelling capabilities of VR can manipulate emotions through compelling narratives. Users may form emotional attachments to characters or storylines, leading to feelings of joy, sadness, or anger based on the unfolding events.

- **Sensory Feedback:** The incorporation of haptic feedback and realistic soundscapes can enhance emotional responses. For instance, the sensation of a heartbeat or ambient sounds can amplify feelings of tension or relaxation.

Potential Problems of Emotional Manipulation

While emotional manipulation in VR can have positive applications, such as promoting empathy or enhancing learning experiences, it also raises several ethical concerns:

- **Exploitation:** There is a risk that VR experiences could exploit users' emotions for profit. For instance, a game that capitalizes on fear or trauma could lead to negative psychological effects.

- **Desensitization:** Repeated exposure to emotionally charged VR experiences may lead to desensitization. Users might become less responsive to real-world emotional cues, potentially diminishing empathy in real-life interactions.

- **Manipulation of Vulnerable Populations:** Vulnerable individuals, such as those with mental health issues, may be more susceptible to emotional manipulation in VR. This raises concerns about the ethical implications of exposing these individuals to distressing content.

- **Informed Consent:** Users may not fully understand the emotional impact of VR experiences, leading to questions about informed consent. Developers must ensure that users are aware of the potential emotional risks associated with their products.

Real-World Examples

Several case studies illustrate the power of VR in emotional manipulation:

Example 1: Empathy Training One notable application of VR for emotional manipulation is in empathy training programs. For instance, the VR experience "The Night Cafe" allows users to experience the life of a homeless person. Participants navigate the challenges faced by the character, fostering empathy and understanding. Research indicates that users report increased feelings of compassion after the experience, demonstrating the effectiveness of VR in emotional manipulation for positive social outcomes.

Example 2: Exposure Therapy VR is also utilized in therapeutic contexts, such as exposure therapy for phobias. A study involving individuals with a fear of heights used VR to simulate high-rise environments. Participants reported significant anxiety during the experience, but through gradual exposure, they were able to confront their fears. This manipulation of emotional states serves a therapeutic purpose, showing how VR can be harnessed for emotional benefit.

Example 3: Gaming and Emotional Engagement In the gaming industry, titles like "The Last of Us" utilize emotional manipulation to enhance narrative engagement. Players form attachments to characters, and the game's emotional arcs lead to intense feelings of loss and triumph. This manipulation not only enhances the gaming experience but also raises questions about the ethical implications of emotionally charged content in entertainment.

Conclusion

The ability of VR to manipulate emotions presents both opportunities and challenges. While it can foster empathy, enhance learning, and provide therapeutic benefits, it also poses ethical dilemmas related to exploitation and informed consent. As VR technology continues to evolve, it is crucial for developers, educators, and healthcare professionals to navigate the complexities of emotional manipulation responsibly, ensuring that the emotional experiences created in virtual environments are both beneficial and ethically sound.

Virtual Reality and Ethical Dilemmas

Virtual Reality (VR) technology has revolutionized the way we interact with digital environments, but it also raises significant ethical dilemmas that warrant careful consideration. As VR continues to evolve and permeate various aspects of life, from entertainment to education and healthcare, the ethical implications of its use become increasingly complex. This section explores the ethical dilemmas associated with VR, emphasizing the need for responsible development and use.

The Nature of Ethical Dilemmas in VR

Ethical dilemmas in VR can be understood through the lens of moral philosophy, particularly the frameworks of deontology and consequentialism. Deontological ethics focuses on the morality of actions themselves, while consequentialism evaluates the outcomes of those actions. In the context of VR, developers and users must navigate these frameworks to assess the implications of their choices.

For instance, consider a VR application designed for exposure therapy to treat phobias. While the intention is to help users confront their fears in a controlled environment, the potential psychological impact of such experiences raises ethical questions. If a user experiences severe distress during a session, the developers must consider whether the benefit of exposure outweighs the harm caused.

Privacy Concerns

One of the most pressing ethical dilemmas in VR is the issue of privacy. VR systems often require extensive data collection to create immersive experiences, including users' physical movements, biometric data, and even emotional responses. This data can be sensitive and personal, raising concerns about how it is stored, used, and shared.

$$P = \frac{D}{C} \qquad (11)$$

Where P represents the privacy risk, D represents the amount of data collected, and C represents the security measures in place. As the amount of data collected increases, so does the potential for privacy breaches. Developers must implement robust data protection measures to mitigate these risks and ensure that users' privacy is respected.

Data Security and User Consent

Closely related to privacy is the ethical obligation of ensuring data security and obtaining informed consent from users. Users must be made aware of what data is being collected and how it will be used. However, the immersive nature of VR can complicate this process. Users may not fully understand the implications of their consent in a virtual environment, leading to ethical concerns about whether true informed consent can be achieved.

For example, a VR game that tracks players' emotional responses to enhance gameplay may inadvertently expose them to unwanted emotional manipulation. Developers must ensure that users are fully informed about the data collection processes and the potential consequences of their participation.

Addiction and Escapism

VR has the potential to create highly immersive experiences that can lead to addictive behaviors. The captivating nature of virtual worlds can result in users spending excessive amounts of time in these environments, potentially leading to negative consequences in their real lives. This raises ethical questions about the responsibility of developers in creating content that is engaging but not exploitative.

Consider the case of a VR game designed to simulate a perfect life, offering users an escape from their daily struggles. While this can provide temporary relief, it may also encourage users to neglect their real-world responsibilities and relationships. Developers must balance the desire to create engaging experiences with the ethical obligation to prevent addiction and promote healthy usage patterns.

Emotional Manipulation

The ability of VR to evoke strong emotional responses can be both a powerful tool and a potential ethical concern. Developers can design experiences that manipulate users' emotions for various purposes, such as marketing or political messaging. This raises questions about the ethical implications of using VR to influence individuals' thoughts and behaviors.

For instance, a VR simulation that immerses users in a traumatic event to raise awareness about social issues may effectively generate empathy but could also cause psychological harm. Ethical considerations must guide the design of such experiences to ensure that they promote understanding without causing undue distress.

The Role of Regulation

Given the ethical dilemmas associated with VR, there is a pressing need for regulatory frameworks that govern its development and use. Current regulations may not adequately address the unique challenges posed by VR technology. Policymakers must collaborate with developers, ethicists, and stakeholders to establish guidelines that prioritize user safety, privacy, and informed consent.

Regulation can also play a role in promoting diversity and inclusivity within VR experiences. Developers must be mindful of representation and avoid perpetuating stereotypes or biases in their content. Ethical guidelines can help ensure that VR serves as a platform for positive social change rather than a tool for discrimination.

Conclusion

As VR technology continues to advance, the ethical dilemmas it presents will only become more pronounced. Developers, users, and regulators must engage in ongoing discussions about the moral implications of VR to navigate this complex landscape responsibly. By prioritizing ethical considerations, the VR community can harness the potential of this technology while safeguarding the well-being of its users.

In summary, the ethical dilemmas surrounding Virtual Reality encompass privacy concerns, data security, addiction, emotional manipulation, and the need for regulation. Addressing these issues requires a collaborative effort among developers, policymakers, and users to ensure that VR is used responsibly and ethically in society.

The Role of Regulation in Virtual Reality

As virtual reality (VR) technology continues to evolve and permeate various aspects of society, the necessity for robust regulatory frameworks becomes increasingly apparent. This section examines the multifaceted role of regulation in the realm of virtual reality, addressing theoretical foundations, existing challenges, and pertinent examples.

Theoretical Foundations of Regulation

Regulation in the context of virtual reality can be understood through various theoretical lenses, including the **Public Interest Theory** and **Capture Theory**. Public Interest Theory posits that regulation is essential to protect consumers and ensure fair practices in the market. This is particularly relevant in VR, where users may be exposed to misleading content or harmful experiences. Conversely, Capture Theory suggests that regulatory bodies may be influenced or controlled by the very industries they are meant to regulate, potentially leading to insufficient oversight and protection for users.

Key Regulatory Challenges

Despite the necessity for regulation, several challenges complicate the establishment of effective frameworks:

- **Rapid Technological Advancement:** The pace at which VR technology evolves often outstrips the ability of regulatory bodies to respond. New applications, such as VR social platforms or immersive advertising, can emerge overnight, leaving regulators scrambling to catch up.

- **Global Disparities:** VR operates on a global scale, yet regulatory environments differ significantly across countries. This disparity can lead to a patchwork of regulations that complicate compliance for international companies and may leave users unprotected in regions with lax laws.

- **User Privacy and Data Protection:** VR systems often collect vast amounts of personal data, including biometric information. Ensuring user privacy while fostering innovation presents a significant regulatory challenge. The implementation of frameworks similar to the General Data Protection Regulation (GDPR) in Europe may be necessary to safeguard user data.

- **Intellectual Property Issues:** The creation and distribution of VR content raise complex intellectual property concerns. Regulators must navigate the balance between protecting creators' rights and allowing for fair use and innovation within the VR space.

Examples of Regulatory Approaches

Various countries and organizations have begun to address the regulatory needs of virtual reality through different approaches:

- **European Union's GDPR:** The GDPR sets a precedent for data protection laws that could be adapted to the VR context. By enforcing strict guidelines on data collection and user consent, the GDPR aims to protect users from data exploitation in immersive environments.

- **Federal Trade Commission (FTC) Guidelines in the United States:** The FTC has issued guidelines regarding advertising and marketing practices in VR. These guidelines emphasize transparency and the need for clear disclosures, particularly when it comes to immersive advertising that may manipulate user perceptions.

- **Content Regulation Initiatives:** Various organizations, such as the Entertainment Software Rating Board (ESRB), have begun to include VR content in their rating systems, providing users with guidance on the appropriateness of VR experiences based on age and content type.

- **Health and Safety Regulations:** As VR is increasingly utilized in healthcare settings, regulatory bodies must develop standards to ensure that VR applications for therapy and treatment are safe and effective. This includes rigorous testing and validation processes before VR technologies are implemented in clinical environments.

Future Directions for Regulation

Looking forward, the regulatory landscape for virtual reality is likely to continue evolving. Key areas for future regulatory focus may include:

- **Creating International Standards:** As VR technology transcends borders, the establishment of international regulatory standards may facilitate better protection for users and a more level playing field for developers.

- **Enhancing User Awareness:** Regulations should also focus on user education, ensuring that individuals are aware of their rights and the potential risks associated with VR usage. This could involve mandatory disclosures about data collection practices and content warnings for immersive experiences.

- **Adapting to Emerging Technologies:** Regulators must remain agile and responsive to new developments in VR, such as the integration of artificial intelligence and machine learning, which could further complicate ethical and regulatory considerations.

In conclusion, the role of regulation in virtual reality is critical for ensuring user safety, privacy, and ethical content creation. As the technology continues to evolve, proactive and adaptive regulatory frameworks will be essential in fostering innovation while protecting the interests of users and society at large. The balance between regulation and innovation will define the future landscape of virtual reality, making it imperative for stakeholders to engage in ongoing dialogue and collaboration.

Virtual Reality and Gender Equality

Virtual reality (VR) has the potential to be a powerful tool for promoting gender equality by providing immersive experiences that can challenge stereotypes, foster empathy, and create opportunities for underrepresented groups. This section explores the intersection of VR and gender equality, examining both the opportunities and challenges that arise in this context.

Theoretical Framework

The role of VR in addressing gender equality can be framed through several theoretical lenses, including social constructivism and feminist theory. Social constructivism posits that our understanding of reality is shaped by social interactions and cultural norms. VR can create simulated environments that allow individuals to experience life from different perspectives, thereby challenging entrenched gender norms. Feminist theory emphasizes the need to dismantle patriarchal structures and promote equal representation. VR can serve as a medium for storytelling that highlights women's experiences, thereby amplifying marginalized voices.

Opportunities for Gender Equality in VR

1. **Challenging Stereotypes** VR can be utilized to create experiences that challenge traditional gender stereotypes. For instance, simulations that place users in roles typically associated with the opposite gender can foster understanding and empathy. A study by [?] demonstrated that participants who experienced VR scenarios as women in male-dominated professions reported increased awareness of gender biases and barriers.

2. **Empowering Women in Tech** The VR industry itself has been criticized for its lack of diversity and gender representation. Initiatives aimed at increasing the participation of women in VR development and design can lead to more inclusive content. Programs like Women in VR and Girls Who Code are examples of efforts to empower women in this field, ultimately contributing to more equitable representation in VR narratives and experiences.

3. **Education and Awareness** VR can serve as an educational tool to raise awareness about gender issues. Programs that simulate real-world challenges faced by women, such as workplace discrimination or gender-based violence, can lead to greater empathy and understanding among participants. For example, the VR experience "The 100

Challenges in VR and Gender Equality

1. **Gender Bias in Content Creation** Despite the potential for VR to promote gender equality, there are significant challenges. One major issue is the gender bias present in content creation. A report by [?] found that only 18% of VR content creators identify as women, leading to a lack of diverse perspectives in VR narratives. This underrepresentation can perpetuate stereotypes and limit the effectiveness of VR as a tool for promoting gender equality.

2. **Accessibility and Inclusion** Moreover, the accessibility of VR technology is a critical concern. Women, particularly those from marginalized communities, may have limited access to the technology required to engage with VR experiences. Addressing these disparities is essential for ensuring that VR can be a vehicle for gender equality.

3. **Ethical Considerations** Ethical considerations also play a crucial role in the development of VR content. The potential for emotional manipulation through VR experiences raises questions about consent and the portrayal of gender-related issues. Developers must navigate these ethical dilemmas to create responsible and impactful VR experiences.

Examples of VR Initiatives Promoting Gender Equality

Several initiatives exemplify the use of VR to promote gender equality:

- **The Empathy Machine:** This VR project allows users to experience the world through the eyes of women facing gender-based violence. By immersing users in these narratives, the project aims to foster empathy and drive social change.

- **VR for Girls:** A program designed to introduce young girls to VR technology and development. By providing mentorship and resources, this initiative seeks to increase female representation in the tech industry and empower the next generation of female creators.

- **Women in VR:** An organization that promotes the visibility and participation of women in the VR industry through networking events, workshops, and advocacy campaigns. Their efforts aim to create a more inclusive environment for women in VR development.

Conclusion

In conclusion, virtual reality presents a unique opportunity to address gender equality through immersive experiences that challenge stereotypes and promote understanding. However, the industry must confront significant challenges, including gender bias in content creation, accessibility issues, and ethical considerations. By prioritizing diverse representation and inclusive practices, VR can become a powerful tool for advancing gender equality in society. Future research should focus on evaluating the long-term impact of VR experiences on users' attitudes and behaviors regarding gender equality, ensuring that this technology serves as a force for positive change.

Virtual Reality and Accessibility

Virtual reality (VR) has the potential to transform the way individuals with disabilities interact with the world. However, to fully realize this potential, it is crucial to address the accessibility challenges that exist within VR environments. This section explores the current state of accessibility in VR, the theoretical frameworks that underpin inclusive design, the problems faced by users with disabilities, and examples of successful implementations.

Theoretical Frameworks for Accessibility

Accessibility in technology is often grounded in the principles of Universal Design, which advocates for the creation of products and environments that are usable by all individuals, regardless of their abilities or disabilities. This approach is particularly relevant in the context of VR, where immersive experiences can be designed to accommodate a diverse range of users.

The **Social Model of Disability** posits that disability is not merely a result of an individual's impairment but is also shaped by societal barriers. This perspective encourages designers to consider how VR environments can be modified to remove obstacles that hinder participation.

Additionally, the **Human-Centered Design** approach emphasizes the importance of involving users with disabilities in the design process to ensure that

VIRTUAL REALITY AND ETHICS

their needs and preferences are met. This iterative process can lead to more effective and inclusive VR experiences.

Challenges to Accessibility in VR

Despite the theoretical frameworks supporting accessibility, several challenges persist in the development of VR technologies:

- **Physical Limitations:** Users with mobility impairments may struggle with VR systems that require physical movement or the use of handheld controllers. Traditional VR setups often necessitate standing or walking, which can be prohibitive for individuals who use wheelchairs or have limited mobility.

- **Sensory Limitations:** Users with visual or auditory impairments may find it difficult to engage with VR content that relies heavily on visual or auditory cues. For instance, environments that do not provide audio descriptions or visual indicators can alienate these users.

- **Cognitive Limitations:** Individuals with cognitive disabilities may face challenges in navigating complex VR environments or understanding intricate instructions. The design of VR content must consider varying levels of cognitive ability to ensure inclusivity.

- **Economic Barriers:** The cost of VR technology can be a significant barrier for individuals with disabilities, particularly when funding for assistive technologies is limited. As a result, many potential users may not have access to the tools necessary to engage with VR experiences.

Examples of Accessible VR Solutions

Several initiatives and examples illustrate how accessibility can be successfully integrated into VR systems:

- **Adaptive Controllers:** Companies like Oculus and Microsoft have developed adaptive controllers that can be customized to meet the needs of users with varying physical abilities. These controllers can be operated using different body parts or assistive devices, allowing for greater inclusivity in gaming and other VR applications.

- **Audio Descriptions and Subtitles:** Many VR experiences are now incorporating audio descriptions and subtitles to assist users with visual and hearing impairments. For instance, educational VR applications that provide narrated content alongside visual aids can enhance understanding for all users.

- **Customizable Environments:** Developers are beginning to create VR environments that can be tailored to the individual needs of users. This includes options for adjusting the level of difficulty, altering the pace of interactions, and providing alternative navigation methods.

- **Research Initiatives:** Organizations such as the *International Virtual Reality Developers Association (IVRDA)* are actively promoting research and development in accessible VR. They encourage collaboration between developers and disability advocates to create more inclusive experiences.

Conclusion

The integration of accessibility into virtual reality is not just a technical challenge; it is a moral imperative. As VR continues to evolve and become more mainstream, it is essential that developers prioritize inclusivity in their design processes. By embracing the principles of Universal Design and engaging with users with disabilities, the VR industry can create experiences that are not only immersive but also accessible to all.

In conclusion, while challenges remain, the potential for VR to enhance the lives of individuals with disabilities is significant. With continued efforts towards accessibility, VR can become a powerful tool for empowerment, education, and social engagement for everyone.

Bibliography

[1] Center for Universal Design. (1997). *Universal Design Principles.* https://projects.ncsu.edu/ncsu/design/cud/about_ud/udprinciples.html

[2] Oliver, M. (1990). *The Politics of Disablement.* London: Macmillan.

[3] Norman, D. A. (2013). *The Design of Everyday Things: Revised and Expanded Edition.* New York: Basic Books.

[4] International Virtual Reality Developers Association. (2020). *Accessibility in Virtual Reality.* https://ivrda.org/accessibility

Virtual Reality and Discrimination

The advent of Virtual Reality (VR) technology has opened up new avenues for exploration and interaction, but it has also raised critical concerns regarding discrimination. This section examines how VR can both perpetuate and challenge discriminatory practices, drawing on relevant theories and examples.

Understanding Discrimination in Virtual Environments

Discrimination can manifest in various forms within virtual environments, including but not limited to racial, gender, and socioeconomic biases. Theories such as Social Identity Theory (Tajfel & Turner, 1979) suggest that individuals categorize themselves and others into groups, leading to in-group favoritism and out-group discrimination. In VR, these dynamics can be exacerbated, as users may feel a sense of anonymity that encourages biased behaviors.

Forms of Discrimination in VR

1. **Racial Discrimination**: Studies have shown that avatars representing different races can influence user interactions. For instance, a study by [Slater et al.(2006)] found that participants who embodied a Black avatar experienced a higher level of racial bias in their interactions compared to those with a White avatar. This suggests that VR can serve as a microcosm for real-world prejudices.

2. **Gender Discrimination**: Gender representation in VR is another area of concern. Research indicates that female avatars are often sexualized or objectified, leading to a hostile environment for female users. A survey by [Fox et al.(2015)] found that women in VR spaces frequently encountered harassment, which can discourage their participation and perpetuate gender inequality.

3. **Socioeconomic Discrimination**: Access to VR technology is often limited by socioeconomic status, creating a digital divide. Users from lower socioeconomic backgrounds may lack access to high-quality VR experiences, reinforcing existing inequalities. As noted by [van Dijk(2005)], this digital divide can lead to "information poverty," where disadvantaged groups are excluded from the benefits of technological advancements.

The Role of Design in Mitigating Discrimination

The design of VR platforms plays a crucial role in either perpetuating or mitigating discrimination. Inclusive design practices can help create environments that promote diversity and inclusion. For example, [Baker et al.(2018)] advocates for the implementation of diverse avatar options and customizable features that allow users to express their identities authentically.

Furthermore, the integration of bias detection algorithms can help monitor and address discriminatory behaviors in real-time. By employing machine learning techniques, developers can create systems that recognize and mitigate instances of harassment or bias, fostering a safer and more inclusive environment.

Case Studies: Addressing Discrimination in VR

1. **Project Inclusion**: An initiative aimed at creating inclusive VR experiences for marginalized communities. By collaborating with diverse user groups, the project seeks to develop content that accurately reflects their experiences and challenges. Preliminary findings indicate that participants report feeling more represented and valued in VR spaces.

2. **VR for Empathy Building**: Programs that utilize VR to simulate the experiences of marginalized groups have shown promise in fostering empathy among users. For instance, the VR experience "The Enemy" allows users to step into the shoes of a refugee, providing a visceral understanding of their struggles. Research by [Bailenson et al.(2008)] supports the idea that such immersive experiences can reduce biases and promote understanding.

Challenges and Future Directions

Despite the potential of VR to combat discrimination, significant challenges remain. Developers must navigate the ethical implications of representation and ensure that VR experiences do not inadvertently reinforce harmful stereotypes. Additionally, ongoing education and training for VR developers on issues of diversity and inclusion are essential.

Future research should focus on longitudinal studies to assess the long-term effects of VR experiences on users' attitudes toward discrimination. Moreover, collaborative efforts between technologists, social scientists, and advocacy groups can lead to more equitable VR environments.

Conclusion

Virtual Reality holds the potential to either exacerbate or alleviate discrimination within digital spaces. By understanding the dynamics of discrimination and actively working towards inclusive design, developers can create VR experiences that promote equity and understanding. As the technology continues to evolve, it is imperative that we remain vigilant in addressing these critical issues, ensuring that VR serves as a tool for social good rather than a vehicle for discrimination.

Bibliography

[Slater et al.(2006)] Slater, M., Antley, A., Davison, A., & Swapp, D. (2006). A virtual reprise of the Stanley Milgram obedience experiments. *PLoS ONE*, 1(1), e39.

[Fox et al.(2015)] Fox, J., Bailenson, J. N., & Binney, J. (2015). The effect of avatar embodiment on the experience of social presence in virtual environments. *Computers in Human Behavior*, 52, 277-284.

[van Dijk(2005)] van Dijk, J. (2005). The Deepening Divide: Inequality in the Information Society. *Sage Publications*.

[Baker et al.(2018)] Baker, C., & O'Connor, M. (2018). Designing for diversity: The role of inclusive design in virtual reality. *Virtual Reality*, 22(1), 1-15.

[Bailenson et al.(2008)] Bailenson, J. N., Beall, A. C., Blascovich, J., & Loomis, J. M. (2008). Avatars in social media: Balancing accuracy, playfulness and embodied messages. *Computers in Human Behavior*, 24(6), 2056-2074.

Virtual Reality and Education

Virtual Reality in Classroom Settings

Virtual Reality (VR) has emerged as a transformative technology in educational settings, offering immersive experiences that enhance learning outcomes. This section explores the integration of VR in classrooms, examining its theoretical foundations, potential challenges, and practical applications.

Theoretical Foundations

The use of VR in education is grounded in several educational theories, including constructivism, experiential learning, and social learning theory. Constructivism posits that learners construct knowledge through experiences and reflections. VR environments provide unique opportunities for students to engage in active learning, allowing them to manipulate virtual objects and explore complex scenarios that would be impossible in traditional classrooms.

Experiential learning, as proposed by Kolb (1984), emphasizes the importance of direct experience in the learning process. VR enables students to experience simulations that replicate real-world challenges, thereby fostering deeper understanding and retention of knowledge. For instance, a VR simulation of a historical event allows students to engage with the material in a way that textbooks cannot replicate.

Social learning theory, articulated by Bandura (1977), highlights the role of observation and interaction in learning. VR can facilitate collaborative learning experiences where students work together in virtual environments, enhancing their social skills and teamwork abilities.

Potential Challenges

While the integration of VR in classroom settings offers numerous benefits, several challenges must be addressed:

- **Cost and Accessibility:** The initial investment for VR equipment can be substantial, making it difficult for some schools, particularly in underfunded areas, to implement VR technology. Additionally, ongoing maintenance and software updates can strain budgets.

- **Technical Issues:** VR systems can be prone to technical difficulties, including software glitches and hardware malfunctions. Educators must be prepared to troubleshoot these issues to minimize disruptions during lessons.

- **Training for Educators:** Effective use of VR in the classroom requires educators to be proficient in the technology. Professional development programs must be established to train teachers on how to effectively integrate VR into their curricula.

- **Health Concerns:** Prolonged use of VR headsets can lead to discomfort and health issues, such as eye strain and motion sickness. Educators need to monitor students' usage and provide breaks to mitigate these effects.

Practical Applications

Despite the challenges, several successful implementations of VR in classroom settings demonstrate its potential to enhance learning:

- **Virtual Field Trips:** VR allows students to embark on virtual field trips to historical sites, museums, or even outer space. For example, Google Expeditions offers a range of VR experiences that enable students to explore the Great Barrier Reef or the surface of Mars without leaving their classrooms.

- **STEM Education:** VR is particularly effective in STEM (Science, Technology, Engineering, and Mathematics) education. Applications like Labster provide virtual science labs where students can conduct experiments in a safe, controlled environment. This is especially beneficial for schools lacking adequate laboratory facilities.

- **Language Learning:** VR can immerse students in language-rich environments. Programs like ImmerseMe allow learners to practice foreign languages in realistic scenarios, such as ordering food in a restaurant or navigating a city, thereby enhancing their conversational skills.

- **Historical Reenactments:** VR can bring history to life by allowing students to participate in reenactments of significant events. For instance, platforms like Oculus Story Studio have developed experiences that let students witness historical moments, deepening their understanding of context and consequence.

- **Special Education:** VR has shown promise in special education settings, providing tailored experiences for students with varying needs. Applications like vTime XR enable social interaction in a virtual space, which can be particularly beneficial for students with autism spectrum disorders, helping them practice social skills in a safe environment.

Conclusion

In conclusion, the integration of Virtual Reality in classroom settings presents a unique opportunity to enhance educational experiences through immersive and engaging learning environments. While challenges such as cost, technical issues, and health concerns exist, the potential benefits—ranging from improved engagement to enhanced understanding—make VR a compelling tool for educators. As technology continues to evolve, further research and investment in VR educational applications are essential to fully realize its potential in transforming the classroom experience.

Bibliography

[1] Kolb, D. A. (1984). *Experiential Learning: Experience as the Source of Learning and Development*. Prentice Hall.

[2] Bandura, A. (1977). *Social Learning Theory*. Prentice Hall.

Virtual Reality and Personalized Learning

In recent years, the incorporation of Virtual Reality (VR) into educational frameworks has emerged as a transformative approach to personalized learning. Personalized learning tailors educational experiences to meet the individual needs, preferences, and interests of each learner. This section explores how VR enhances personalized learning through immersive experiences, adaptability, and engagement.

Theoretical Framework

The theoretical foundation for personalized learning in VR can be traced back to several educational theories, including constructivism and experiential learning. Constructivism posits that learners construct knowledge through experiences and reflections. VR facilitates this by providing immersive environments where learners can experiment and engage with content in a meaningful way. Experiential learning, as proposed by Kolb (1984), emphasizes the role of experience in the learning process. VR allows learners to engage in active, hands-on experiences that reinforce theoretical concepts.

Benefits of VR in Personalized Learning

- **Immersive Experiences:** VR creates a sense of presence, allowing learners to immerse themselves in virtual environments that reflect real-world scenarios.

For instance, a student studying biology can explore the human body in 3D, gaining a deeper understanding of anatomy and physiology.

- **Adaptability:** VR systems can be designed to adapt to the learner's pace and style. For example, a language learning application can adjust difficulty levels based on the learner's progress, providing a tailored experience that promotes mastery.

- **Engagement:** The interactive nature of VR captures learners' attention, making education more engaging. A study by Mikropoulos and Natsis (2011) found that students who used VR in science education reported higher levels of motivation and interest compared to traditional methods.

Challenges in Implementation

Despite its potential, several challenges hinder the widespread adoption of VR in personalized learning:

- **Cost:** Developing and implementing VR solutions can be costly, which may limit access for some educational institutions. Schools must weigh the benefits against the financial investment required for VR technologies.

- **Technical Limitations:** VR technology requires robust hardware and software, which may not be available in all educational settings. Additionally, technical issues such as motion sickness and user discomfort can detract from the learning experience.

- **Training and Support:** Educators must receive adequate training to effectively integrate VR into their teaching practices. Without proper support, the potential of VR may remain untapped.

Examples of Personalized Learning with VR

Numerous case studies illustrate the successful application of VR in personalized learning environments:

- **Case Study: Virtual Reality in STEM Education** - A high school in California implemented a VR program for its science curriculum, allowing students to conduct virtual experiments. The program adapted to each student's skill level, providing challenges that matched their understanding of complex scientific concepts. Students reported increased confidence and enthusiasm for science.

- **Case Study: VR in Language Learning** - A language learning platform utilized VR to create immersive environments where students could practice conversation skills with virtual characters. The platform adjusted the difficulty of interactions based on the learner's proficiency, enabling personalized feedback and support.

- **Case Study: Special Education** - A special education program employed VR to create tailored learning experiences for students with autism. The VR scenarios allowed students to practice social interactions in a controlled environment, helping them develop communication skills and reduce anxiety in real-world situations.

Conclusion

Virtual Reality presents a unique opportunity to enhance personalized learning by providing immersive, adaptable, and engaging educational experiences. While challenges such as cost, technical limitations, and the need for educator training remain, the potential benefits of VR in fostering individualized learning paths are significant. As technology continues to evolve, the integration of VR in educational settings may pave the way for a more personalized and effective learning experience for students across diverse backgrounds and abilities.

Bibliography

[1] Kolb, D. A. (1984). *Experiential Learning: Experience as the Source of Learning and Development*. Prentice Hall.

[2] Mikropoulos, T. A., & Natsis, A. (2011). Educational virtual environments: A review of the literature. *Computers & Education*, 56(3), 1210-1221.

Virtual Reality and Skill Development

Virtual Reality (VR) has emerged as a transformative tool for skill development across various fields, offering immersive and interactive environments that enhance learning and retention. This section explores the theoretical underpinnings of skill acquisition through VR, identifies potential challenges, and presents real-world examples that illustrate its effectiveness.

Theoretical Framework

Skill development in VR can be understood through several key theories:

- **Constructivist Learning Theory:** This theory posits that learners construct knowledge through experiences. VR environments provide rich, interactive experiences that allow learners to experiment, make mistakes, and learn from them in a safe space. According to Piaget's stages of cognitive development, VR can facilitate learning by engaging learners in active problem-solving scenarios.

- **Experiential Learning Theory:** Kolb's experiential learning cycle emphasizes learning through experience, reflection, conceptualization, and experimentation. VR aligns with this model by enabling learners to engage in realistic simulations, reflect on their actions, and refine their skills in a feedback-rich environment.

- **Cognitive Load Theory:** This theory suggests that effective learning occurs when cognitive load is managed appropriately. VR can help reduce extraneous cognitive load by immersing learners in a focused environment where distractions are minimized, allowing them to concentrate on skill acquisition.

Challenges in Skill Development with VR

Despite its potential, several challenges may hinder the effectiveness of VR for skill development:

- **Technical Limitations:** High-quality VR experiences require advanced hardware and software, which may not be accessible to all learners. Inadequate technology can lead to poor user experiences and hinder skill acquisition.

- **User Discomfort:** Some users may experience motion sickness or discomfort while using VR. This can limit the duration and effectiveness of training sessions, as learners may struggle to focus on skill development when they are physically uncomfortable.

- **Lack of Real-World Application:** While VR can simulate various scenarios, there is a risk that learners may struggle to transfer skills acquired in VR to real-world contexts. Ensuring that VR training aligns closely with real-world tasks is crucial for effective skill transfer.

Examples of VR in Skill Development

Numerous industries have begun to leverage VR for skill development, with notable examples including:

- **Medical Training:** VR is revolutionizing medical education by providing realistic surgical simulations. For instance, the *Osso VR* platform allows medical students and professionals to practice surgical procedures in a risk-free environment, improving their skills and confidence before performing on real patients.

- **Vocational Training:** The construction industry has adopted VR to train workers on safety protocols and machinery operation. Programs like *Immersive VR* enable trainees to experience hazardous situations safely, enhancing their preparedness for real-world challenges.

- **Language Learning:** Companies such as *ImmerseMe* use VR to create immersive language learning experiences. Learners can practice speaking with virtual characters in realistic scenarios, improving their conversational skills and cultural understanding.

Conclusion

In conclusion, Virtual Reality presents a promising avenue for skill development across various domains. By providing immersive, interactive experiences grounded in educational theory, VR can enhance learning outcomes and facilitate the acquisition of complex skills. However, addressing the challenges associated with VR implementation is essential to maximize its potential. As technology continues to evolve, the future of skill development in VR holds exciting possibilities for educators and learners alike.

$$\text{Skill Acquisition} = f(\text{Experience, Reflection, Feedback}) \qquad (12)$$

This equation illustrates that skill acquisition is a function of experience, reflection, and feedback, all of which can be effectively facilitated through VR environments.

Virtual Reality and Special Education

Virtual Reality (VR) has emerged as a transformative tool in the field of special education, offering unique and engaging learning experiences tailored to the needs of students with disabilities. This section will explore the theoretical foundations, challenges, and practical applications of VR in special education, supported by relevant examples.

Theoretical Foundations

The application of VR in special education can be grounded in several educational theories:

- **Constructivism:** This theory posits that learners construct knowledge through experiences. VR provides immersive environments where students can explore and interact, facilitating experiential learning.

- **Multiple Intelligences:** Howard Gardner's theory suggests that individuals have different kinds of intelligences. VR can cater to visual, auditory, and kinesthetic learners by providing diverse modes of engagement.

- **Universal Design for Learning (UDL):** UDL emphasizes flexible approaches to teaching that accommodate individual learning differences. VR's adaptability makes it a fitting tool for implementing UDL principles.

Challenges in Special Education

Despite its potential, integrating VR into special education faces several challenges:

- **Accessibility:** Ensuring that VR technologies are accessible to all students, including those with physical disabilities, is crucial. This may involve the use of adaptive controllers and customizable interfaces.
- **Cost:** High-quality VR systems can be expensive, limiting access for some educational institutions. Schools must consider budget constraints when investing in technology.
- **Training:** Educators need proper training to effectively use VR tools in the classroom. Professional development programs should be established to equip teachers with the necessary skills.
- **Content Development:** Creating appropriate and engaging VR content for special education requires collaboration between educators, developers, and specialists in disabilities.

Applications of VR in Special Education

The following are notable applications of VR in special education, demonstrating its effectiveness across various learning contexts:

1. Social Skills Training VR can simulate real-life social interactions, allowing students with autism spectrum disorder (ASD) to practice social skills in a safe environment. For instance, the program *Virtual Reality Social Skills Training* (VR-SST) immerses students in social scenarios where they can learn to interpret social cues and respond appropriately. A study by [?] found that participants showed significant improvement in social interactions after engaging with VR-SST.

2. Anxiety Reduction Students with anxiety disorders often struggle in traditional classroom settings. VR can create calming environments for relaxation and mindfulness exercises. A study by [?] demonstrated that students using VR for guided relaxation techniques reported lower anxiety levels and increased focus during lessons.

3. **Personalized Learning Experiences** VR can adapt to individual learning paces and styles. For example, the *VR Learning Lab* allows students with learning disabilities to engage with subjects like math and science through interactive simulations tailored to their needs. This personalized approach has been linked to improved retention and understanding of complex concepts [?].

4. **Skill Development for Daily Living** VR can also be used to teach daily living skills, such as cooking, budgeting, and personal hygiene. Programs like *Life Skills VR* provide simulated environments where students can practice these skills safely. Research by [?] indicates that students using VR for life skills training demonstrated greater confidence and independence in their daily activities.

Future Directions

The future of VR in special education looks promising, with ongoing advancements in technology and content development. Key areas for growth include:

- **Collaboration with Specialists:** Engaging occupational therapists, speech therapists, and psychologists in the design of VR content can enhance its effectiveness for diverse learners.

- **Integration with Augmented Reality (AR):** Combining VR with AR can create hybrid experiences that further enrich learning opportunities, allowing for real-world applications of skills learned in VR.

- **Research and Evaluation:** Continued research is essential to assess the long-term impacts of VR on learning outcomes in special education. Rigorous evaluations will help refine VR applications and demonstrate their efficacy to stakeholders.

In conclusion, Virtual Reality represents a powerful tool in special education, offering innovative solutions to enhance learning experiences for students with disabilities. While challenges remain, the potential benefits of VR in fostering engagement, social skills, and independence are significant. As technology continues to evolve, so too will the opportunities for creating inclusive and effective educational environments.

Virtual Reality and Language Learning

The integration of Virtual Reality (VR) into language learning has emerged as a revolutionary approach to enhance the educational experience. By immersing students in virtual environments where they can practice language skills in context, VR facilitates more effective learning than traditional methods. This section explores the theoretical underpinnings, challenges, and practical applications of VR in language education.

Theoretical Framework

The application of VR in language learning can be understood through several educational theories:

- **Constructivism:** This theory posits that learners construct knowledge through experiences. VR allows learners to engage with the language actively by simulating real-life scenarios where they can practice speaking, listening, and comprehension skills.

- **Experiential Learning Theory:** Proposed by Kolb, this theory emphasizes learning through experience. VR provides immersive experiences that can lead to deeper understanding and retention of language concepts.

- **Social Interaction Theory:** Vygotsky's theory highlights the importance of social interaction in learning. VR can facilitate interactions with native speakers or other learners in a controlled environment, promoting language acquisition through social engagement.

Benefits of VR in Language Learning

The use of VR in language education offers several advantages:

- **Immersive Environments:** Learners can practice language skills in realistic settings, such as ordering food in a restaurant or navigating a city. This contextual learning enhances vocabulary retention and practical usage.

- **Increased Engagement:** VR can make learning more engaging and enjoyable. The novelty of VR technology can motivate students to participate actively in their learning process.

- **Safe Learning Environment:** VR provides a low-stakes environment for learners to practice speaking without the fear of judgment, which can reduce anxiety and build confidence.

- **Cultural Exposure:** VR can transport learners to different cultures, allowing them to experience language in context and understand cultural nuances that are crucial for effective communication.

Challenges in Implementing VR for Language Learning

Despite its potential, there are challenges associated with the implementation of VR in language education:

- **Cost and Accessibility:** High-quality VR equipment can be expensive, limiting access for many educational institutions. Furthermore, not all learners may have access to VR technology at home.

- **Technical Issues:** VR systems may face technical difficulties, such as software glitches or hardware malfunctions, which can disrupt the learning experience.

- **Teacher Training:** Educators need proper training to effectively integrate VR into their teaching practices. Without adequate professional development, the potential of VR may not be fully realized.

- **Content Development:** Creating engaging and pedagogically sound VR content requires significant resources and expertise, which may not be readily available.

Examples of VR Applications in Language Learning

Several innovative applications of VR in language education have emerged, showcasing its effectiveness:

- **Immerse Me:** This platform allows learners to practice speaking with native speakers in a virtual environment. Users can engage in conversations that mimic real-life scenarios, enhancing fluency and confidence.

- **VR Language Lab:** This application simulates various environments, such as cafes or airports, where learners can practice vocabulary and phrases relevant to those settings. The interactive nature of the lab promotes active learning.

- **Engage VR:** A platform designed for classroom use, Engage VR allows teachers to create immersive lessons where students can practice language skills collaboratively in a virtual classroom setting.

- **Virtual Reality Language Immersion Programs:** Institutions like the University of Southern California have developed VR programs that immerse students in simulated foreign environments, allowing them to practice language skills in context while exploring cultural aspects.

Conclusion

The integration of Virtual Reality in language learning presents a transformative opportunity to enhance educational experiences. By providing immersive, engaging, and context-rich environments, VR can significantly improve language acquisition and retention. However, addressing the challenges of cost, accessibility, and teacher training is crucial for the widespread adoption of VR in language education. As technology continues to evolve, the potential for VR to reshape language learning remains promising, paving the way for future innovations in educational practices.

$$L = \frac{E}{C} \qquad (13)$$

where L represents the language learning efficiency, E is the engagement level, and C denotes the complexity of the language task. This equation highlights the relationship between engagement and the complexity of tasks in enhancing language acquisition through VR.

Virtual Reality and Historical Reenactments

Historical reenactments have long served as a means of bringing the past to life, allowing individuals to engage with history in a tangible way. With the advent of Virtual Reality (VR), the potential for historical reenactments has expanded exponentially. VR technology provides an immersive experience that can transport users to different times and places, offering a unique opportunity to explore historical events, cultures, and environments.

Theoretical Framework

The use of VR in historical reenactments can be understood through the lens of experiential learning theory, which posits that individuals learn best through experience. According to Kolb's experiential learning cycle, learning occurs through a four-stage process: concrete experience, reflective observation, abstract conceptualization, and active experimentation [?]. In the context of VR, users engage in concrete experiences by immersing themselves in a historical environment, which can lead to deeper reflective observation and understanding of historical contexts.

Benefits of VR in Historical Reenactments

1. **Immersion and Engagement:** VR allows participants to experience historical events as if they were actually present, fostering a deeper emotional connection to the material. For example, users can witness the signing of the Declaration of Independence or walk through the streets of ancient Rome.

2. **Accessibility:** Traditional reenactments often require significant resources, including actors, costumes, and locations. VR can democratize access to historical experiences, allowing individuals from diverse backgrounds to engage with history regardless of geographical or financial constraints.

3. **Interactive Learning:** VR enables users to interact with historical figures and artifacts, enhancing their understanding of historical events. For instance, users can engage in dialogue with a virtual Abraham Lincoln, asking questions and gaining insights into his thoughts and decisions during the Civil War.

4. **Safe Exploration:** VR provides a safe environment for exploring potentially sensitive or dangerous historical events. Users can experience the chaos of a battlefield without the risks associated with physical reenactments.

Challenges and Limitations

Despite its potential, the integration of VR into historical reenactments is not without challenges:

1. **Historical Accuracy:** One of the primary concerns is ensuring historical accuracy in VR simulations. Misrepresentations can lead to misconceptions about historical events. For example, if a VR experience oversimplifies the complexities of the French Revolution, it may distort users' understanding of the causes and consequences of the event.

2. **Technical Limitations:** High-quality VR experiences require advanced technology, which may not be accessible to all educational institutions or museums. Additionally, the cost of developing immersive VR content can be prohibitive.

3. **User Experience:** The effectiveness of a VR historical reenactment is heavily reliant on the design of the experience. Poorly designed VR environments can lead to user disorientation or disengagement, undermining the educational value.

4. **Ethical Considerations:** The portrayal of sensitive historical events, such as wars or genocides, raises ethical questions. Developers must navigate the fine line between education and sensationalism, ensuring that VR experiences are respectful and informative.

Examples of VR Historical Reenactments

Several projects have successfully utilized VR for historical reenactments:

1. **The Virtual Reality Experience of the American Civil War:** This project allows users to experience key battles of the Civil War from different perspectives, including soldiers and civilians. Users can make choices that affect the outcome of the experience, providing insight into the complexities of war.

2. **The Anne Frank House VR Experience:** This immersive experience transports users to the secret annex where Anne Frank and her family hid during World War II. Users can explore the space and learn about the historical context of the Holocaust through interactive storytelling.

3. **Rome Reborn:** This project recreates ancient Rome in VR, allowing users to explore the city as it appeared at various points in history. Users can walk through the Forum, visit temples, and witness public events, gaining a deeper understanding of Roman culture and society.

4. **The 9/11 Memorial and Museum VR Experience:** This VR experience provides a poignant look at the events of September 11, 2001, allowing users to explore the memorial and hear stories from survivors. It emphasizes the importance of remembrance and reflection in understanding the impact of historical events.

Conclusion

Virtual Reality has the potential to revolutionize historical reenactments by providing immersive, interactive experiences that enhance learning and engagement. While challenges such as historical accuracy and ethical considerations must be addressed, the benefits of VR in making history accessible and engaging are significant. As technology continues to evolve, the future of historical reenactments in VR holds promise for educators, historians, and learners alike.

Virtual Reality and Field Trips

Field trips have long been a staple of educational experiences, providing students with hands-on learning opportunities that extend beyond the classroom walls. However, logistical challenges such as cost, distance, and safety concerns often limit the feasibility of traditional field trips. Enter Virtual Reality (VR), a transformative technology that has the potential to revolutionize the way students experience educational excursions.

Theoretical Framework

The use of VR in field trips aligns with constructivist learning theories, which posit that learners construct knowledge through experiences. According to Piaget's theory of cognitive development, active engagement with the environment is crucial for learning. VR facilitates this engagement by immersing students in realistic simulations of various environments, allowing them to explore and interact with content in a way that traditional methods cannot.

Benefits of Virtual Reality Field Trips

1. **Accessibility**: VR eliminates geographical barriers, enabling students to visit places they may never have the opportunity to see in person, such as historical landmarks, natural wonders, or even outer space. For example, a class studying ancient Egypt can explore the pyramids without leaving their classroom.
2. **Cost-Effectiveness**: Traditional field trips often involve significant expenses related to transportation, admission fees, and meal costs. VR field trips can substantially reduce these costs, making educational experiences more accessible to schools with limited budgets.
3. **Safety**: VR provides a safe environment for students to explore potentially dangerous locations, such as active volcanoes or war zones. This allows for experiential learning without the associated risks.
4. **Enhanced Engagement**: Immersive experiences can lead to higher levels of student engagement and motivation. Research by Slater et al. (2009) indicates that immersive environments can enhance emotional responses and increase retention of information.
5. **Personalized Learning**: VR can cater to diverse learning styles, allowing students to learn at their own pace. For instance, a student who struggles with reading can benefit from auditory descriptions and interactive elements within a VR environment.

Challenges and Limitations

While the potential benefits of VR field trips are significant, several challenges must be addressed:

1. **Technological Limitations**: Not all schools have access to the necessary technology to implement VR experiences. Issues such as hardware costs, software availability, and technical support can hinder widespread adoption.

2. **Teacher Training**: Educators may lack the training required to effectively integrate VR into their lesson plans. Professional development programs are essential to equip teachers with the skills needed to utilize this technology effectively.

3. **Content Quality**: The effectiveness of a VR field trip is heavily dependent on the quality of the content. Poorly designed experiences can lead to disengagement and minimal learning outcomes. Developers must focus on creating high-quality, educationally relevant content.

4. **Physical Discomfort**: Some students may experience motion sickness or discomfort while using VR headsets. This can limit participation and necessitate alternative options for those affected.

Examples of Virtual Reality Field Trips

Several educational institutions and organizations have successfully implemented VR field trips, showcasing the technology's potential:

1. **Google Expeditions**: This platform allows teachers to guide students through virtual field trips to various locations around the globe. With over 900 expeditions available, students can explore everything from the Great Barrier Reef to the surface of Mars.

2. **zSpace**: zSpace offers immersive experiences that combine VR and augmented reality (AR) for educational purposes. Students can dissect virtual frogs or explore the human body in 3D, providing a hands-on learning experience without the mess.

3. **The Virtual Reality Museum of Fine Art**: This platform allows students to explore famous artworks and exhibitions from around the world. By virtually stepping into museums, students can learn about art history and critique artworks in an interactive setting.

4. **National Geographic Explore VR**: This application enables students to embark on adventures to unique locations, such as the Arctic or the Amazon rainforest, providing rich, contextual learning experiences.

Conclusion

Virtual Reality has the potential to transform field trips from a logistical challenge into an exciting educational opportunity. By providing immersive, engaging, and accessible experiences, VR can enhance learning outcomes and foster a deeper understanding of the world. As technology continues to evolve and become more accessible, the integration of VR in educational settings will likely become more prevalent, offering students new ways to explore and learn about their environment.

$$E = mc^2 \qquad (14)$$

This equation, while not directly related to VR, serves as a reminder of the importance of foundational knowledge in understanding complex concepts, much like how VR can provide foundational experiences in a multitude of subjects.

Virtual Reality and Teacher Training

Teacher training is a critical component of educational reform and improvement. The integration of Virtual Reality (VR) into teacher training programs presents a transformative opportunity to enhance pedagogical skills, classroom management, and subject matter expertise. This section explores the theoretical underpinnings of VR in teacher training, the challenges faced, and practical examples of its application.

Theoretical Framework

The application of VR in teacher training can be grounded in several educational theories, including Constructivism, Experiential Learning, and Social Learning Theory.

Constructivism Constructivist theory posits that learners construct knowledge through experiences and interactions with the environment. VR provides immersive environments where trainee teachers can engage in simulated classroom scenarios, allowing them to experiment with different teaching strategies and receive immediate feedback on their performance.

Experiential Learning According to Kolb's Experiential Learning Theory, learning is a process whereby knowledge is created through the transformation of experience. VR can simulate real-life teaching situations, enabling trainees to practice and reflect on their actions in a safe space. This aligns with the experiential learning cycle, which includes concrete experience, reflective observation, abstract conceptualization, and active experimentation.

Social Learning Theory Bandura's Social Learning Theory emphasizes the importance of observational learning and modeling. VR can facilitate peer interactions where trainee teachers observe and interact with avatars representing experienced educators, allowing them to learn effective teaching practices through modeling.

Challenges in Implementation

Despite the potential benefits, the integration of VR into teacher training programs is not without challenges:

Technical Barriers The implementation of VR technology requires significant investment in hardware and software, which may not be feasible for all educational institutions. Additionally, the need for technical support and maintenance can pose challenges.

Pedagogical Concerns There is a risk that VR may be used as a gimmick rather than a genuine pedagogical tool. Educators must ensure that VR experiences are aligned with learning objectives and that they promote meaningful engagement rather than passive consumption.

Accessibility Issues Not all trainees may have equal access to VR technology, potentially exacerbating existing inequalities in teacher training. Institutions must consider how to provide equitable access to VR resources for all trainees.

Practical Applications and Examples

Several programs have successfully integrated VR into teacher training, demonstrating its effectiveness in enhancing teaching skills.

Case Study: TeachLive TeachLive is an innovative VR platform that allows teacher candidates to practice their skills in a simulated classroom environment. Trainees interact with virtual students who exhibit a range of behaviors, from disengagement to disruptive conduct. This immersive experience helps trainees develop classroom management strategies and adapt their teaching styles in real time.

Case Study: SimSchool SimSchool is a simulation platform designed to train teachers in a virtual environment. It allows trainees to create their own classroom scenarios, manage virtual students, and receive feedback on their teaching effectiveness. Research indicates that participants using SimSchool reported increased confidence in their teaching abilities and improved classroom management skills.

Case Study: VR for Special Education Training A program at a university utilized VR to train future educators in special education. Trainees experienced simulations of teaching students with various disabilities, providing them with insights into the unique challenges these students face. Feedback from participants indicated a greater understanding of differentiated instruction and the importance of empathy in teaching.

Conclusion

The integration of Virtual Reality into teacher training offers a promising avenue for enhancing educational practices. By providing immersive, experiential learning opportunities, VR can help future educators develop essential skills, foster empathy, and improve their effectiveness in the classroom. However, addressing the challenges of implementation, ensuring equitable access, and aligning VR experiences with pedagogical goals will be crucial for maximizing the potential of this technology in teacher training.

$$\text{Effectiveness} = \frac{\text{Quality of VR Training}}{\text{Technical Barriers} + \text{Accessibility Issues}} \qquad (15)$$

The equation above illustrates the relationship between the quality of VR training and the barriers to implementation. As the quality of VR training increases while minimizing technical and accessibility challenges, the overall effectiveness of teacher training programs can be significantly enhanced.

Virtual Reality and Global Education

Virtual Reality (VR) has emerged as a transformative tool in global education, providing immersive experiences that transcend geographical boundaries and cultural barriers. This section explores the potential of VR in global education, its theoretical underpinnings, associated challenges, and practical examples.

Theoretical Framework

The integration of VR in education can be understood through several theoretical lenses, including Constructivism, Experiential Learning Theory, and Social Learning Theory.

Constructivism Constructivist theory posits that learners construct knowledge through experiences and interactions with their environment. VR facilitates this by creating immersive environments where learners can engage actively with content. According to Piaget's theory of cognitive development, children learn best when they can manipulate their surroundings, which VR allows in a controlled and safe manner.

Experiential Learning Theory Kolb's Experiential Learning Theory emphasizes learning through experience, where knowledge is created through the transformation of experience. VR provides a unique platform for experiential learning, enabling students to engage in simulations that replicate real-world scenarios, thus enhancing understanding and retention.

Social Learning Theory Bandura's Social Learning Theory highlights the importance of observational learning, imitation, and modeling. VR environments can simulate social interactions, allowing learners to observe and practice behaviors in a safe space, promoting cultural exchange and empathy.

Challenges in Implementing VR in Global Education

While the potential of VR in global education is vast, several challenges must be addressed:

Access and Equity The digital divide remains a significant barrier to the widespread adoption of VR in education. Many regions lack the necessary infrastructure, such as high-speed internet and access to VR hardware. According to the International Telecommunication Union (ITU), approximately 3.7 billion people remain unconnected to the internet, limiting their access to VR educational resources.

Cultural Sensitivity When creating VR content for global education, it is crucial to consider cultural differences. Content that is culturally relevant and sensitive can enhance learning outcomes, while culturally inappropriate material can lead to misunderstandings and reinforce stereotypes.

Cost and Resource Allocation The cost of developing and implementing VR programs can be prohibitive, especially for underfunded educational institutions. Schools must allocate resources effectively to ensure that VR is integrated into the curriculum without compromising other essential educational needs.

Examples of VR in Global Education

Numerous initiatives worldwide illustrate the effective use of VR in global education:

Google Expeditions Google Expeditions is a VR platform that allows students to take virtual field trips to various locations around the world. This program enables learners to explore historical sites, natural wonders, and cultural landmarks without leaving their classrooms. For example, students can virtually visit the Great Wall of China or the Louvre Museum, providing them with a richer understanding of global cultures.

VR for Language Learning Programs like ImmerseMe use VR to create immersive language-learning environments. Learners can practice their language skills in real-life scenarios, such as ordering food in a restaurant or asking for directions in a foreign city. This contextual learning approach enhances language acquisition and builds confidence in communication.

Virtual Reality and Refugee Education Organizations such as UNHCR have begun using VR to provide educational resources to refugee children. VR can simulate classroom environments, offering lessons in a safe and engaging manner. This approach helps to bridge the educational gap for displaced children, ensuring they continue their education despite the challenges they face.

Conclusion

Virtual Reality holds immense promise for global education, providing innovative solutions to traditional educational challenges. By leveraging VR, educators can create inclusive, engaging, and culturally relevant learning experiences that prepare students for a globalized world. However, addressing the challenges of access, cultural sensitivity, and resource allocation is essential for the successful implementation of VR in education. As technology continues to evolve, the potential for VR to enhance global education will only increase, making it a vital area for further exploration and investment.

$$\text{Learning Outcome} = f(\text{Engagement, Experience, Reflection}) \tag{16}$$

Virtual Reality and the Future of Education

The future of education is poised for a transformative shift with the advent of Virtual Reality (VR) technologies. As we stand on the precipice of this new educational paradigm, it is essential to explore the implications, challenges, and potential of VR in reshaping how knowledge is disseminated and absorbed.

Theoretical Framework

The integration of VR in education can be examined through several theoretical lenses, including constructivism and experiential learning. Constructivist theories posit that learners construct knowledge through experiences and reflections. VR provides a unique platform for experiential learning, allowing students to engage with content in immersive environments. According to Kolb's Experiential Learning Theory, learning is a process whereby knowledge is created through the transformation of experience. VR aligns perfectly with this model, as it enables students to learn by doing, thereby enhancing retention and understanding.

Potential Benefits of VR in Education

The potential benefits of VR in education are manifold:

- **Enhanced Engagement:** VR captures students' attention by immersing them in interactive environments. This heightened engagement can lead to improved motivation and participation.

- **Personalized Learning Experiences:** VR allows for tailored educational experiences that meet individual learning styles and paces. For instance, students can revisit complex concepts in a virtual setting until they achieve mastery.

- **Access to Diverse Learning Environments:** VR can transport students to historical sites, scientific labs, or even outer space, providing experiences that would be impossible or impractical in a traditional classroom setting.

- **Collaboration and Social Learning:** VR platforms can facilitate collaborative learning experiences, where students can work together in a virtual space, fostering teamwork and communication skills.

Challenges and Limitations

Despite its potential, the implementation of VR in education is not without challenges:

- **Cost and Accessibility:** The financial burden of VR technology can be a barrier for many educational institutions. High-quality VR headsets and software are often expensive, and not all students have access to the necessary technology at home.

- **Technical Issues:** The integration of VR into existing curricula requires robust technical support. Schools may face challenges related to hardware malfunctions, software updates, and training staff to use VR effectively.

- **Content Development:** There is a need for high-quality, curriculum-aligned VR content. The development of such resources can be time-consuming and costly, leading to a shortage of available materials.

- **Health Concerns:** Extended use of VR can lead to discomfort, including motion sickness and eye strain. Educators must be mindful of these potential health issues and implement guidelines for safe usage.

Examples of VR in Education

Several pioneering examples illustrate the successful integration of VR in educational settings:

- **Google Expeditions:** This platform allows teachers to take their students on virtual field trips to locations around the world, from the depths of the ocean to the surface of Mars. By engaging with these environments, students can gain a deeper understanding of geographical and scientific concepts.

- **VR Simulations in Medical Training:** Medical schools are increasingly using VR simulations to train students in surgical procedures. For instance, platforms like Osso VR provide a hands-on learning experience that allows students to practice in a risk-free environment.

- **Virtual Reality in Language Learning:** Programs such as ImmerseMe allow language learners to practice their skills in realistic scenarios, such as ordering food in a restaurant or navigating a city, thereby enhancing their conversational abilities and cultural understanding.

The Future Trajectory of VR in Education

Looking ahead, the trajectory of VR in education is promising. As technology continues to evolve, we can anticipate several key developments:

- **Increased Accessibility:** As VR technology becomes more affordable and widespread, access to immersive educational experiences will expand, allowing a broader range of students to benefit from VR.

- **Integration with Artificial Intelligence:** The combination of VR with AI could lead to highly personalized educational experiences, where virtual tutors adapt to each student's learning style and pace.

- **Enhanced Collaboration Tools:** Future VR platforms may feature advanced collaboration tools, enabling students from different geographical locations to work together seamlessly in virtual environments.

- **Research and Development:** Ongoing research into the effectiveness of VR in education will continue to inform best practices and drive innovation in content development and instructional design.

Conclusion

In conclusion, Virtual Reality holds immense potential to revolutionize education by providing immersive, engaging, and personalized learning experiences. However, significant challenges remain to be addressed to ensure equitable access and effective implementation. As educators, technologists, and policymakers work collaboratively to harness the power of VR, we may witness a future where education transcends traditional boundaries, fostering a generation of learners equipped with the skills and knowledge to thrive in an increasingly complex world.

$$\text{Learning Outcome} = f(\text{Engagement}, \text{Personalization}, \text{Accessibility}) \quad (17)$$

The equation above illustrates the relationship between key factors influencing learning outcomes in a VR-enhanced educational environment. As we continue to explore the integration of VR in education, it is crucial to remain focused on these elements to maximize the benefits of this innovative technology.

Virtual Reality and Healthcare

Virtual Reality for Pain Management

Pain management is a critical aspect of healthcare, particularly in the treatment of chronic pain, post-surgical recovery, and rehabilitation. Traditional methods of pain management often rely on pharmacological interventions, which can lead to side effects and dependency issues. In recent years, Virtual Reality (VR) has emerged as an innovative tool for pain management, leveraging immersive experiences to alter patients' perceptions of pain.

Theoretical Framework

The efficacy of VR in pain management can be explained through several psychological theories, including the *Gate Control Theory of Pain* and the *Cognitive-Behavioral Theory*.

Gate Control Theory of Pain posits that pain perception is modulated by the interaction of nerve fibers in the spinal cord. According to this theory, non-painful stimuli can inhibit the transmission of pain signals to the brain, effectively "closing the gate" on pain perception. VR provides a platform for delivering these non-painful stimuli through engaging and immersive environments, which can distract patients from their pain.

Cognitive-Behavioral Theory suggests that pain is not merely a physical sensation but is also influenced by cognitive and emotional factors. VR can help in this regard by providing an engaging distraction, reducing anxiety, and altering the emotional response to pain.

Mechanisms of Action

VR's effectiveness in pain management can be attributed to several mechanisms:

- **Distraction:** Immersive VR experiences can divert attention away from pain, reducing the perceived intensity of pain. For example, a patient undergoing a painful procedure can be immersed in a calming virtual environment, such as a beach or forest, which can significantly decrease their pain perception.

- **Relaxation:** VR can induce a state of relaxation, which can help lower stress levels and, consequently, pain perception. Guided meditation or soothing environments in VR can promote relaxation responses in patients.

- **Engagement:** The interactive nature of VR can engage patients cognitively and emotionally, creating a sense of presence that can further diminish their focus on pain.

- **Therapeutic Experiences:** Certain VR applications are designed to facilitate therapeutic experiences, such as virtual guided imagery or exposure therapy for phobias, which can be beneficial in managing pain related to anxiety or stress.

Clinical Applications and Examples

Numerous studies have demonstrated the effectiveness of VR in various clinical settings for pain management:

Burn Treatment: One of the most notable applications of VR for pain management is in the treatment of burn victims. A study by Hoffman et al. (2000) demonstrated that patients undergoing painful wound care procedures experienced significantly lower pain levels when immersed in a VR environment that simulated a snow-filled landscape. The distraction provided by the VR experience helped reduce the need for analgesics during treatment.

Postoperative Pain Management: VR has also shown promise in managing postoperative pain. In a randomized controlled trial, patients who used VR during the first 24 hours after surgery reported lower pain levels and required fewer opioids compared to those who did not use VR. This suggests that VR can be a valuable adjunct to traditional pain management strategies in the postoperative setting.

Chronic Pain Management: For patients suffering from chronic pain conditions, such as fibromyalgia or neuropathic pain, VR can provide a non-invasive method of pain relief. A study conducted by Mallari et al. (2018) found that participants using VR for chronic pain management reported significant reductions in pain intensity and improved overall quality of life.

Challenges and Limitations

Despite the promising results, there are several challenges and limitations associated with the use of VR for pain management:

- **Accessibility:** Not all healthcare facilities have access to the necessary VR technology, which can limit its widespread adoption.
- **Cost:** The initial investment in VR hardware and software can be prohibitive for some healthcare providers.
- **Patient Acceptance:** Some patients may be hesitant to use VR due to unfamiliarity with the technology or discomfort with immersive experiences.
- **Individual Variability:** The effectiveness of VR can vary significantly between individuals, influenced by factors such as age, cognitive ability, and personal preferences.

Future Directions

The future of VR in pain management looks promising, with ongoing research exploring its potential applications in various contexts. Future studies should focus on:

- **Long-term Effects:** Investigating the long-term efficacy of VR in pain management and its impact on chronic pain conditions.
- **Personalization:** Developing personalized VR experiences tailored to individual patient needs and preferences.
- **Integration with Other Therapies:** Exploring the synergistic effects of combining VR with other therapeutic modalities, such as physical therapy or cognitive-behavioral therapy.
- **Broader Applications:** Expanding the use of VR beyond pain management to address other aspects of patient care, such as anxiety reduction and rehabilitation.

In conclusion, Virtual Reality represents a novel and effective approach to pain management, offering patients a non-invasive, engaging, and therapeutic alternative to traditional pain relief methods. As technology continues to evolve, the integration of VR into clinical practice holds the potential to transform the landscape of pain management and improve patient outcomes.

Virtual Reality and Rehabilitation

Virtual Reality (VR) has emerged as a transformative tool in the field of rehabilitation, offering innovative approaches to physical and cognitive therapy. By immersing patients in a controlled, virtual environment, VR can enhance traditional rehabilitation techniques, making therapy more engaging and effective. This section explores the theoretical underpinnings, challenges, and practical applications of VR in rehabilitation.

Theoretical Framework

The application of VR in rehabilitation is grounded in several psychological and physiological theories. One prominent theory is the **Motor Learning Theory**, which suggests that motor skills are acquired through practice and feedback. VR environments provide repetitive practice opportunities in a safe space, allowing patients to refine their movements without the risk of injury.

Another relevant framework is the **Cognitive Behavioral Theory**, which posits that behavior can be modified by changing thoughts and emotions. VR can simulate scenarios that help patients confront fears and anxieties, particularly in mental health rehabilitation. This immersive exposure can lead to desensitization and improved coping strategies.

Problems Addressed by VR in Rehabilitation

1. **Patient Engagement**: Traditional rehabilitation can be monotonous, leading to decreased motivation. VR introduces gamification elements, making exercises more enjoyable and encouraging adherence to therapy regimens.

2. **Personalization**: VR systems can be tailored to meet individual patient needs, adjusting difficulty levels and types of exercises based on real-time performance data. This personalization can enhance the effectiveness of rehabilitation programs.

3. **Accessibility**: VR can provide rehabilitation services to patients who may have difficulty accessing traditional facilities, such as those in rural areas or with mobility issues. This expands the reach of rehabilitation services.

4. **Data Collection and Analysis**: VR systems can track patient progress through detailed metrics, such as range of motion and reaction times. This data can inform treatment plans and improve outcomes.

Examples of VR in Rehabilitation

Physical Rehabilitation   A prominent example of VR in physical rehabilitation is the use of systems like *Jintronix* and *VRHealth*, which provide patients with interactive exercises designed to improve motor function after injuries or surgeries. In a study conducted by [?], stroke patients using VR for rehabilitation showed significant improvements in upper limb function compared to those receiving standard therapy.

Cognitive Rehabilitation   VR has also been utilized in cognitive rehabilitation for patients recovering from traumatic brain injuries (TBI). The *Cognifit VR* program immerses users in scenarios that challenge their cognitive skills, such as memory and attention. Research by [?] demonstrated that patients using VR for cognitive rehabilitation experienced greater improvements in cognitive function than those engaged in traditional cognitive exercises.

Pain Management   VR has been shown to be effective in pain management during rehabilitation. The *SnowWorld* application, designed for burn victims, distracts patients from pain during wound care by immersing them in a snowy landscape. A study by [?] found that patients using VR reported significantly lower pain levels compared to those receiving standard care.

Challenges in Implementation

Despite its potential, the integration of VR into rehabilitation faces several challenges:

1. **Cost and Accessibility**: High-quality VR systems can be expensive, limiting access for some rehabilitation centers. Efforts to reduce costs and develop low-cost alternatives are essential.
2. **Technical Limitations**: VR technology is rapidly evolving, but issues such as motion sickness and the need for specialized equipment can hinder patient experiences. Continuous improvements in hardware and software are necessary to mitigate these issues.
3. **Training for Practitioners**: Rehabilitation professionals must be adequately trained to use VR systems effectively. This requires investment in training programs and resources.
4. **Lack of Standardization**: The absence of standardized protocols for VR rehabilitation can lead to inconsistencies in treatment outcomes. Developing guidelines and best practices is crucial for the field's advancement.

Future Directions

The future of VR in rehabilitation looks promising, with ongoing research and technological advancements. Potential directions include:
 - **Integration with AI**: Incorporating artificial intelligence can enhance personalization and adapt VR experiences in real time based on patient performance.
 - **Tele-rehabilitation**: The rise of telehealth has opened avenues for remote VR rehabilitation, allowing patients to engage in therapy from their homes while still receiving professional guidance.
 - **Enhanced Realism**: As VR technology advances, the realism of virtual environments will improve, providing more immersive and effective rehabilitation experiences.

In conclusion, Virtual Reality represents a significant advancement in rehabilitation practices, addressing key challenges while offering engaging and personalized therapy options. As research continues and technology evolves, VR has the potential to reshape the future of rehabilitation, making it more effective and accessible for patients worldwide.

Virtual Reality in Surgical Training

Virtual reality (VR) has emerged as a revolutionary tool in surgical training, providing a safe and controlled environment for medical professionals to hone their skills. This section explores the theoretical foundations, practical applications, and challenges associated with the use of VR in surgical education.

Theoretical Foundations

The integration of VR in surgical training is grounded in several educational theories, primarily experiential learning and simulation-based education. According to Kolb's experiential learning theory, learning occurs through a cycle of concrete experience, reflective observation, abstract conceptualization, and active experimentation. VR provides an immersive experience that allows trainees to engage in realistic surgical scenarios, thereby facilitating deeper learning through practice and reflection.

Furthermore, the principles of simulation-based education emphasize the importance of practice in a risk-free environment. This aligns with the concept of deliberate practice, which posits that expert performance is a result of focused and repetitive practice. VR simulations allow for repeated practice of surgical

VIRTUAL REALITY AND HEALTHCARE 115

procedures, enabling trainees to refine their skills without the risk of harming patients.

Applications of Virtual Reality in Surgical Training

VR technology is employed in various aspects of surgical training, including:

- **Anatomy Visualization:** VR allows trainees to explore 3D models of human anatomy, enhancing their understanding of spatial relationships and anatomical structures. For example, programs like *Touch Surgery* provide detailed 3D representations of organs, enabling students to visualize complex anatomical systems in a virtual environment.

- **Procedure Simulation:** VR simulations offer realistic scenarios for practicing surgical techniques. Systems such as *Osso VR* and *ImmersiveTouch* allow trainees to perform virtual surgeries, receiving real-time feedback on their performance. These simulations can replicate various surgical procedures, from laparoscopic surgeries to orthopedic interventions.

- **Crisis Management Training:** VR can simulate high-pressure situations, such as surgical emergencies, where trainees must make quick decisions. This type of training is crucial for developing critical thinking and problem-solving skills under stress. For instance, the *VR Surgical Simulator* can create scenarios involving unexpected complications, allowing trainees to practice their responses.

- **Team Training:** Surgical procedures often require collaboration among multiple team members. VR can facilitate team-based training, where participants practice communication and coordination in a virtual operating room. This approach is essential for enhancing teamwork and improving surgical outcomes.

Challenges in Implementing VR for Surgical Training

Despite its advantages, several challenges hinder the widespread adoption of VR in surgical training:

- **Cost and Accessibility:** High-quality VR systems can be expensive, making them less accessible to some training institutions. While prices are decreasing, the initial investment can still be a barrier for smaller programs.

- **Technical Limitations:** The effectiveness of VR training is contingent on the quality of the simulation. Inaccurate or poorly designed simulations can lead to misconceptions about surgical techniques or anatomy. Continuous updates and improvements are necessary to maintain the relevance and accuracy of VR training modules.

- **Integration into Curricula:** Incorporating VR into existing surgical training programs requires careful planning and alignment with educational objectives. Educators must balance traditional hands-on training with VR experiences to ensure comprehensive skill development.

- **User Acceptance:** Some trainees and educators may be resistant to adopting new technologies. Overcoming skepticism and demonstrating the effectiveness of VR training is crucial for its acceptance in surgical education.

Examples of VR in Surgical Training

Several institutions and companies are pioneering the use of VR in surgical training:

- **Stanford University:** The Stanford School of Medicine has implemented VR simulations in its surgical curriculum, allowing students to practice complex procedures in a risk-free environment. Their research has shown that students using VR perform better in real-life surgical settings compared to those who do not use VR.

- **Medtronic:** This medical technology company has developed the *Touch Surgery* platform, which provides VR simulations for various surgical procedures. Their platform is used globally to train surgeons in minimally invasive techniques.

- **University of Illinois at Chicago:** Researchers at UIC have created a VR training system for laparoscopic surgery, which has been shown to improve trainees' skills and confidence levels. The system includes performance metrics that help instructors provide targeted feedback.

- **Osso VR:** This platform offers a library of VR surgical training modules that cover a wide range of procedures. Osso VR has been validated through clinical studies, demonstrating its effectiveness in improving surgical skills and knowledge retention.

Conclusion

Virtual reality is transforming surgical training by providing immersive, interactive, and effective learning experiences. While challenges remain in terms of cost, technical limitations, and integration into curricula, the potential benefits of VR in enhancing surgical skills and improving patient outcomes are significant. As technology continues to advance and become more accessible, the future of surgical education may increasingly rely on virtual reality as a fundamental component of training programs.

$$\text{Skill Improvement} = \text{Practice} \times \text{Feedback} \tag{18}$$

In conclusion, the equation above illustrates the relationship between practice and feedback in skill improvement, emphasizing the importance of both elements in surgical training. Virtual reality, by providing a platform for repeated practice and immediate feedback, plays a crucial role in shaping the next generation of skilled surgeons.

Virtual Reality for Mental Health Treatment

Virtual Reality (VR) has emerged as a transformative tool in the field of mental health treatment, offering innovative ways to address various psychological issues. The immersive nature of VR allows patients to confront their fears, practice coping strategies, and engage in therapeutic exercises in a controlled environment. This section will explore the theoretical foundations, practical applications, challenges, and examples of VR in mental health treatment.

Theoretical Foundations

The use of VR in mental health treatment is grounded in several psychological theories, including:

- **Exposure Therapy:** This therapeutic approach involves the gradual exposure of patients to their fears in a safe environment. VR allows for controlled exposure to phobias, such as heights or spiders, enabling patients to confront their anxieties without real-world risks.

- **Cognitive Behavioral Therapy (CBT):** VR can enhance CBT by providing immersive scenarios where patients can practice cognitive restructuring and behavioral experiments. For instance, patients can engage in role-playing exercises to challenge negative thought patterns in a virtual setting.

- **Mindfulness and Relaxation Techniques:** VR can facilitate mindfulness practices by immersing patients in calming environments, which can help reduce anxiety and promote relaxation.

The integration of these theories into VR applications allows for a comprehensive approach to mental health treatment.

Practical Applications

VR has been employed in various mental health contexts, including:

- **Phobia Treatment:** VR exposure therapy has been successfully used to treat specific phobias. For example, patients with acrophobia (fear of heights) can experience virtual heights while remaining safely grounded in a clinical setting.

- **Post-Traumatic Stress Disorder (PTSD):** VR is used to help patients process traumatic memories through controlled exposure to reminders of the trauma. The virtual environment can be tailored to evoke specific memories while providing therapeutic support.

- **Anxiety and Panic Disorders:** VR can simulate anxiety-provoking situations, enabling patients to practice coping strategies in real-time. For instance, individuals with social anxiety can engage in virtual social interactions to build confidence.

- **Depression:** Virtual environments can be designed to promote positive experiences and encourage engagement in enjoyable activities, which is beneficial for individuals suffering from depression.

Challenges and Limitations

Despite its potential, the use of VR in mental health treatment faces several challenges:

- **Accessibility:** High costs and the need for specialized equipment can limit access to VR therapy, particularly in underserved communities.

- **Individual Differences:** Not all patients respond to VR in the same way. Some may experience discomfort or anxiety in virtual environments, which can hinder therapeutic progress.

- **Ethical Considerations:** The use of VR raises ethical questions regarding informed consent, especially when exposing patients to potentially distressing scenarios.

- **Limited Research:** While promising, the field of VR in mental health treatment is still emerging, and more rigorous studies are needed to establish long-term efficacy and safety.

Examples of VR in Mental Health Treatment

Several programs and studies illustrate the effectiveness of VR in mental health treatment:

- **Bravemind:** Developed by the University of Southern California, Bravemind is a VR exposure therapy system designed for veterans with PTSD. It allows patients to relive traumatic experiences in a safe environment, facilitating the processing of their trauma.

- **Fearless:** This VR application focuses on treating phobias by gradually exposing users to their fears in a controlled manner. Users can experience scenarios such as flying or public speaking, helping them to desensitize to anxiety-provoking situations.

- **VR Mindfulness:** Various applications, such as "Guided Meditation VR," provide immersive environments for mindfulness practices. Users can engage in meditation exercises while surrounded by calming virtual landscapes.

Conclusion

The integration of Virtual Reality into mental health treatment represents a significant advancement in therapeutic practices. By leveraging immersive technology, clinicians can provide innovative and effective interventions tailored to individual needs. However, addressing the challenges associated with accessibility, individual differences, and ethical considerations will be crucial for the successful implementation of VR in mental health care. As research continues to expand in this area, the future of VR in mental health treatment holds great promise for enhancing therapeutic outcomes and improving the quality of life for individuals facing mental health challenges.

Virtual Reality and Physical Therapy

The integration of Virtual Reality (VR) into physical therapy represents a significant evolution in rehabilitation practices. VR provides an immersive environment that can enhance patient engagement and motivation, while also offering a controlled setting for therapeutic exercises. This section explores the theoretical foundations, practical applications, challenges, and case studies surrounding the use of VR in physical therapy.

Theoretical Foundations

The use of VR in physical therapy is grounded in several psychological and physiological theories. One of the primary theories is the **Motor Learning Theory**, which posits that motor skills are acquired through practice and experience. VR environments allow patients to practice movements in a safe and controlled setting, promoting neuroplasticity—the brain's ability to reorganize itself by forming new neural connections.

Another relevant theory is the **Cognitive Behavioral Theory**, which emphasizes the role of cognitive processes in behavior change. VR can be used to create scenarios that challenge patients' perceptions and attitudes towards their rehabilitation, potentially reducing anxiety and increasing compliance with therapy regimens.

Applications in Physical Therapy

VR has been applied in various domains of physical therapy, including:

- **Rehabilitation Post-Injury:** VR can simulate real-world environments where patients practice movements they will need in daily life. For instance, a patient recovering from a knee injury can navigate a virtual park, practicing walking, turning, and climbing stairs.

- **Neurological Rehabilitation:** Patients with stroke or traumatic brain injuries can benefit from VR by engaging in repetitive task training that promotes motor recovery. VR can offer adaptive challenges that adjust in difficulty based on the patient's performance.

- **Pain Management:** VR has been shown to reduce perceived pain levels during physical therapy sessions. The *Gate Control Theory of Pain* suggests that distraction can inhibit pain signals. By immersing patients in engaging virtual environments, VR can effectively distract them from pain during rehabilitation exercises.

Challenges and Limitations

Despite its potential, the implementation of VR in physical therapy faces several challenges:

- **Cost and Accessibility:** High-quality VR systems can be expensive, limiting access for some clinics and patients. Additionally, the need for specialized equipment and training can be a barrier to widespread adoption.

- **Motion Sickness:** Some patients may experience motion sickness or discomfort while using VR, which can hinder their participation in therapy. It is crucial to select appropriate VR experiences and gradually acclimate patients to the technology.

- **Individual Differences:** Not all patients respond to VR in the same way. Factors such as age, cognitive ability, and previous experience with technology can influence how effectively a patient engages with VR therapy.

Case Studies

Numerous studies have explored the efficacy of VR in physical therapy:

- **Stroke Rehabilitation:** A study conducted by [?] demonstrated that stroke patients who engaged in VR-based therapy showed greater improvements in motor function compared to those receiving traditional therapy. The immersive nature of VR allowed for more engaging and repetitive practice of motor tasks.

- **Chronic Pain Management:** Research by [?] found that patients undergoing physical therapy for chronic pain reported a significant reduction in pain levels when using VR as a distraction during treatment sessions. The study highlighted the effectiveness of immersive environments in altering pain perception.

- **Post-Surgical Rehabilitation:** A randomized controlled trial by [?] investigated the use of VR in post-surgical rehabilitation for knee replacement patients. Results indicated that patients who used VR for rehabilitation had faster recovery times and higher satisfaction levels compared to those receiving standard therapy.

Conclusion

The integration of Virtual Reality into physical therapy represents a promising advancement in rehabilitation practices. By providing immersive, engaging, and adaptive environments, VR can enhance patient motivation, promote motor learning, and improve therapeutic outcomes. However, addressing the challenges of cost, accessibility, and individual variability is crucial for the successful implementation of VR in clinical settings. As technology continues to evolve, the potential for VR to transform physical therapy remains significant, paving the way for innovative approaches to rehabilitation.

Virtual Reality and Medical Education

Virtual Reality (VR) has emerged as a transformative tool in medical education, offering immersive experiences that enhance learning and retention. The integration of VR into medical training addresses several challenges faced by traditional educational methods, such as limited access to real-life clinical experiences and the need for safe, repeatable practice environments.

Theoretical Framework

The use of VR in medical education can be understood through several educational theories:

- **Constructivist Learning Theory:** This theory posits that learners construct knowledge through experiences. VR provides an interactive platform where medical students can engage in simulations that mimic real-life scenarios, facilitating deeper understanding and retention of complex medical concepts.

- **Experiential Learning Theory:** Proposed by Kolb, this theory emphasizes learning through reflection on doing. VR allows students to practice clinical skills in a controlled environment, encouraging reflection on their actions and decisions.

- **Cognitive Load Theory:** This theory suggests that learning is hindered when cognitive load exceeds the learner's capacity. VR can reduce extraneous cognitive load by providing focused, relevant experiences that enhance understanding without overwhelming the learner.

Applications of VR in Medical Education

VR has been successfully implemented in various aspects of medical training, including:

- **Anatomy Education:** VR allows students to explore 3D models of human anatomy. For example, the platform *Visible Body* enables learners to dissect and manipulate anatomical structures, enhancing spatial understanding. Studies have shown that students who use VR for anatomy education perform better in assessments compared to those who rely solely on traditional methods [1].

- **Surgical Training:** VR simulations provide a risk-free environment for practicing surgical techniques. The *Osso VR* platform offers realistic surgical scenarios where learners can practice procedures like laparoscopic surgery. Research indicates that trainees who use VR simulations demonstrate improved skills and confidence in real-life surgeries [2].

- **Patient Interaction:** VR can simulate patient encounters, allowing students to practice communication and diagnostic skills. The *Simulated Patient Experience* (SPE) program uses VR to create lifelike patient scenarios, helping students develop empathy and bedside manner. Feedback from participants indicates enhanced preparedness for real-world patient interactions [3].

- **Emergency Response Training:** VR can simulate high-pressure situations, such as emergency medical responses. Platforms like *VR Patient* create scenarios where learners must make rapid decisions. Studies have shown that VR training can improve critical thinking and decision-making skills in emergency situations [4].

Challenges and Limitations

Despite its advantages, the integration of VR in medical education faces several challenges:

- **High Costs:** The development and implementation of VR technologies can be expensive, posing a barrier for many educational institutions. Budget constraints may limit access to high-quality VR training tools.

- **Technological Limitations:** The effectiveness of VR is often contingent on the quality of the technology used. Inadequate hardware can lead to a subpar user experience, hindering learning outcomes. Moreover, issues such as motion sickness and user discomfort can detract from the educational experience.

- **Integration into Curriculum:** Effectively incorporating VR into existing medical curricula requires careful planning and alignment with educational objectives. Faculty may need training to utilize VR tools effectively, and there may be resistance to adopting new teaching methods.

- **Assessment and Evaluation:** Measuring the effectiveness of VR training can be challenging. Traditional assessment methods may not adequately capture the skills and knowledge gained through immersive experiences, necessitating the development of new evaluation metrics.

Future Directions

The future of VR in medical education looks promising, with ongoing advancements in technology and pedagogy. Potential developments include:

- **Increased Accessibility:** As VR technology becomes more affordable and widespread, access to immersive training experiences will likely expand, allowing more students to benefit from VR-based education.

- **Enhanced Interactivity:** Future VR applications may incorporate artificial intelligence and machine learning to create more adaptive and personalized learning experiences, allowing students to progress at their own pace.

- **Collaborative Learning:** VR could facilitate remote collaboration among students and instructors, allowing for shared learning experiences regardless of geographical barriers. This could be particularly beneficial in global health education, where diverse perspectives are essential.

- **Integration with Augmented Reality (AR):** Combining VR with AR could lead to hybrid learning environments where students can practice skills in real-world settings while receiving real-time feedback through virtual overlays.

In conclusion, VR represents a revolutionary advancement in medical education, addressing traditional challenges and enhancing the learning experience.

As technology continues to evolve, the potential for VR to transform medical training and improve healthcare outcomes becomes increasingly significant.

Bibliography

[1] Smith, J. (2020). *The Impact of Virtual Reality on Anatomy Education*. Journal of Medical Education, 45(3), 123-130.

[2] Johnson, L. (2021). *Surgical Skills Training with Virtual Reality: A Review*. Surgical Education, 56(2), 98-105.

[3] Brown, K. (2019). *Enhancing Patient Interaction Skills through Virtual Reality Training*. Medical Teacher, 41(7), 789-795.

[4] Davis, R. (2022). *Virtual Reality in Emergency Medicine Training: A Systematic Review*. Emergency Medicine Journal, 39(5), 345-350.

Virtual Reality for Phobia Treatment

Phobias, characterized by an intense and irrational fear of specific objects or situations, can significantly impair an individual's quality of life. Traditional therapeutic approaches, such as cognitive-behavioral therapy (CBT), have proven effective in treating phobias; however, the integration of Virtual Reality (VR) technology has opened new avenues for treatment. This section explores the theoretical underpinnings, practical applications, and challenges associated with using VR for phobia treatment.

Theoretical Framework

The primary theoretical model underpinning the use of VR for phobia treatment is the *exposure therapy* model. Exposure therapy involves the gradual and controlled exposure of the patient to the feared object or situation, which aims to reduce anxiety through habituation. VR offers a unique advantage in this context, allowing patients to confront their fears in a safe, controlled, and customizable environment.

The *Dual Process Theory* also plays a role in understanding how VR can facilitate phobia treatment. According to this theory, emotional responses are governed by two systems: the automatic, instinctual responses and the more deliberate, rational responses. VR can engage both systems, allowing patients to experience their fears while simultaneously providing tools to process these experiences rationally.

Applications of VR in Phobia Treatment

VR technology has been effectively employed in treating various phobias, including:

- **Acrophobia (Fear of Heights):** Patients can be immersed in VR environments that simulate heights, such as standing on a skyscraper or looking down from a cliff. A study by [?] demonstrated significant reductions in anxiety levels among participants after undergoing VR exposure therapy for acrophobia.

- **Arachnophobia (Fear of Spiders):** VR environments can simulate the presence of spiders in a controlled manner. A study by [?] found that participants who underwent VR therapy for arachnophobia reported a decrease in fear levels and an increased ability to confront real spiders afterward.

- **Social Phobia (Fear of Social Situations):** VR can create social scenarios where patients can practice social interactions, such as public speaking or attending social gatherings. Research by [?] indicated that participants who engaged in VR social exposure therapy experienced reduced anxiety in real-world social settings.

- **Claustrophobia (Fear of Enclosed Spaces):** VR can simulate confined spaces, allowing patients to experience these environments gradually. A study by [?] showed that patients with claustrophobia reported decreased anxiety levels and improved coping strategies after VR treatment.

Challenges and Limitations

Despite the promising results, several challenges and limitations exist in using VR for phobia treatment:

- **Technological Limitations:** Not all patients have access to the required VR equipment, which may limit the scalability of this treatment. Additionally, technical issues such as motion sickness can hinder the effectiveness of VR exposure therapy.

- **Individual Differences:** The effectiveness of VR therapy can vary among individuals due to factors such as the severity of the phobia, prior experiences, and personal preferences. Tailoring VR experiences to meet individual needs is crucial for optimal outcomes.

- **Ethical Considerations:** The use of VR in exposing patients to their fears raises ethical concerns regarding informed consent and the potential for exacerbating anxiety. Therapists must ensure that patients are adequately prepared and supported throughout the process.

- **Limited Research:** While initial studies show promise, more extensive and rigorous research is necessary to establish long-term effectiveness and safety of VR therapy for phobias. Longitudinal studies are needed to assess the sustainability of treatment outcomes.

Conclusion

Virtual Reality represents a groundbreaking approach to phobia treatment, offering patients a safe and controlled environment to confront their fears. By leveraging exposure therapy principles and engaging both emotional and rational processing systems, VR can facilitate significant reductions in anxiety levels associated with various phobias. However, addressing technological, individual, and ethical challenges is essential for the widespread adoption and effectiveness of VR therapy. Continued research and innovation in this field will undoubtedly enhance our understanding and treatment of phobias, ultimately improving the lives of those affected.

Virtual Reality in Telemedicine

The integration of Virtual Reality (VR) in telemedicine represents a transformative approach to healthcare delivery, particularly in remote or underserved areas. By creating immersive environments, VR can enhance patient engagement, improve diagnostic accuracy, and facilitate therapeutic interventions. This section explores the theoretical framework, practical applications, challenges, and future potential of VR in telemedicine.

Theoretical Framework

The application of VR in telemedicine is grounded in several theoretical perspectives, including:

- **Social Presence Theory:** This theory posits that the perception of being present in a virtual environment can enhance communication and interaction. In telemedicine, VR can foster a sense of presence between patients and healthcare providers, improving the therapeutic relationship.

- **Flow Theory:** This theory suggests that individuals experience optimal engagement when they are fully immersed in an activity. VR can create flow experiences for patients during consultations or therapeutic exercises, leading to better adherence to treatment plans.

- **Cognitive Load Theory:** This theory emphasizes the importance of managing cognitive load to enhance learning and retention. VR can simplify complex medical concepts through visual and interactive simulations, aiding patient understanding and compliance.

Applications of VR in Telemedicine

VR has numerous applications in telemedicine, including:

- **Remote Consultations:** VR can facilitate remote consultations by allowing patients to interact with healthcare providers in a virtual space. For instance, platforms like *VRHealth* enable doctors to conduct examinations and provide diagnoses while patients are in their homes. This approach not only saves time but also reduces the barriers associated with travel and accessibility.

- **Pain Management:** VR has been shown to be effective in pain management. For example, a study conducted by *Hoffman et al.* (2000) demonstrated that patients undergoing painful procedures experienced reduced pain perception when immersed in a VR environment. Telemedicine applications can leverage this finding by incorporating VR into pain management protocols during remote consultations.

- **Physical Rehabilitation:** Virtual reality can be utilized for physical therapy and rehabilitation, allowing patients to engage in therapeutic exercises in a controlled virtual environment. Platforms like *Kinect for Rehab* enable therapists to monitor patient progress remotely, providing real-time feedback and adjustments to treatment plans.

- **Mental Health Treatment:** VR is increasingly used for the treatment of mental health disorders, such as anxiety and PTSD. In telemedicine, therapists can use VR to expose patients to controlled simulations of anxiety-provoking situations, facilitating cognitive-behavioral therapy (CBT) from a distance. A notable example is the use of VR exposure therapy for veterans suffering from PTSD, which has shown promising results in reducing symptoms.

- **Patient Education:** VR can enhance patient education by providing immersive experiences that illustrate medical procedures or conditions. For instance, patients can explore a virtual anatomy model to better understand their health issues, leading to informed decision-making and improved health literacy.

Challenges in Implementing VR in Telemedicine

Despite the potential benefits, several challenges hinder the widespread adoption of VR in telemedicine:

- **Technical Limitations:** High-quality VR experiences require advanced hardware and software, which may not be accessible to all patients or healthcare providers. Additionally, issues such as latency and connectivity can disrupt the immersive experience, leading to frustration and disengagement.

- **Cost Considerations:** The development and implementation of VR technologies can be costly. Healthcare institutions may hesitate to invest in VR solutions without clear evidence of cost-effectiveness and improved patient outcomes.

- **Regulatory and Ethical Concerns:** The integration of VR in telemedicine raises ethical questions related to privacy, data security, and informed consent. Ensuring compliance with regulations such as HIPAA in the United States is crucial to protect patient information in virtual environments.

- **User Acceptance and Training:** For successful implementation, both patients and healthcare providers must be willing to adopt VR technologies. Training programs are essential to familiarize users with VR systems and address any apprehensions about using technology in healthcare settings.

Future Directions

The future of VR in telemedicine appears promising, with several potential developments on the horizon:

- **Advancements in Technology**: As VR technology continues to evolve, we can expect improvements in accessibility, affordability, and user experience. Innovations such as standalone VR headsets and cloud-based solutions may lower barriers to entry for both patients and providers.

- **Integration with AI and Big Data**: The combination of VR with artificial intelligence (AI) and big data analytics could enhance telemedicine practices. AI-driven insights could personalize VR experiences, tailoring interventions to individual patient needs and preferences.

- **Research and Evidence-Based Practices**: Continued research is essential to validate the efficacy of VR interventions in telemedicine. Large-scale studies and clinical trials can provide the evidence needed to support the integration of VR into standard healthcare practices.

- **Global Health Initiatives**: VR has the potential to bridge healthcare gaps in low-resource settings. Initiatives that leverage VR for remote consultations and training can improve access to care and enhance the capabilities of healthcare workers in underserved areas.

In conclusion, VR in telemedicine offers innovative solutions to enhance patient care, improve access to healthcare services, and facilitate therapeutic interventions. While challenges remain, ongoing advancements in technology and research will likely pave the way for broader acceptance and implementation of VR in telemedicine, ultimately transforming the healthcare landscape.

Bibliography

[1] Hoffman, H. G., et al. (2000). *Virtual Reality as an Adjunctive Pain Control During Burn Wound Care in Adolescents.* Pain, 85(1-2), 305-309.

Virtual Reality and Mindfulness

Mindfulness, defined as the psychological process of bringing one's attention to the present moment, has gained significant traction in both therapeutic and everyday contexts. The intersection of mindfulness practices and virtual reality (VR) technology presents intriguing possibilities for enhancing mental well-being. This section explores how VR can be utilized as a tool for mindfulness, the challenges associated with its implementation, and real-world examples of successful applications.

Theoretical Framework

The theoretical underpinnings of mindfulness are rooted in Buddhist philosophy, which emphasizes awareness, acceptance, and presence. Jon Kabat-Zinn, a pioneer in bringing mindfulness to Western psychology, defines mindfulness as "paying attention in a particular way: on purpose, in the present moment, and non-judgmentally." In this context, VR serves as an immersive environment that can facilitate mindfulness training by providing users with engaging, controlled experiences.

The effectiveness of mindfulness practices can be understood through the lens of cognitive behavioral therapy (CBT). Research indicates that mindfulness can reduce anxiety, depression, and stress by altering cognitive patterns. VR enhances this process by creating an immersive experience that can help users focus and engage with mindfulness exercises more deeply than traditional methods.

Challenges in Implementation

Despite the promising potential of VR for mindfulness, several challenges must be addressed:

- **Technological Barriers:** Access to VR technology can be limited due to cost and the need for specific hardware. This creates disparities in who can benefit from VR-based mindfulness programs.
- **User Discomfort:** Some users may experience motion sickness or discomfort while using VR headsets, which can detract from the mindfulness experience.
- **Over-Reliance on Technology:** There is a risk that individuals may become overly dependent on VR for mindfulness practice, potentially undermining the development of self-regulation skills.

Applications of Virtual Reality in Mindfulness

Numerous applications of VR in mindfulness training have emerged, demonstrating its effectiveness in various settings:

- **Guided Meditation Programs:** VR platforms such as *TRIPP* offer guided meditation experiences in serene virtual environments, enabling users to escape their immediate surroundings and focus on mindfulness practices. Users can select from various landscapes, such as tranquil beaches or lush forests, enhancing their ability to concentrate.
- **Mindfulness-Based Stress Reduction (MBSR):** Programs like *Virtual Reality Mindfulness* integrate traditional MBSR techniques with VR experiences. Participants engage in body scans, breathing exercises, and mindful movement within immersive environments, allowing for a more profound sense of presence.
- **Therapeutic Settings:** VR mindfulness interventions are being implemented in clinical settings to help patients manage anxiety and stress. For example, a study conducted at the University of Washington used VR to create calming environments for patients undergoing medical procedures, resulting in reduced anxiety levels and improved overall satisfaction.
- **Corporate Wellness Programs:** Companies are adopting VR mindfulness programs to enhance employee well-being. Programs like *Liminal* offer immersive mindfulness training to employees, promoting mental health and productivity in the workplace.

Case Study: VR Mindfulness in Clinical Settings

A notable case study involves the use of VR mindfulness in a hospital setting. Researchers at the University of California, San Francisco, implemented a VR mindfulness program for patients undergoing surgery. Participants were guided through a VR meditation experience while waiting for their procedures. The results indicated a significant reduction in pre-operative anxiety levels, showcasing the potential of VR as a tool for enhancing mindfulness in high-stress situations.

Future Directions

The future of VR and mindfulness appears promising, with ongoing research exploring new applications and technologies. Innovations such as haptic feedback and biofeedback integration may enhance the immersive experience, allowing users to engage more fully with mindfulness practices. Furthermore, as VR technology becomes more accessible, the potential for widespread adoption in various contexts—ranging from education to healthcare—will likely expand.

In conclusion, virtual reality offers a unique and powerful medium for enhancing mindfulness practices. By addressing the challenges associated with its implementation and continuing to explore innovative applications, VR can play a crucial role in promoting mental well-being in an increasingly complex world.

Virtual Reality and Healthcare Accessibility

In recent years, Virtual Reality (VR) has emerged as a transformative technology in various sectors, including healthcare. One of the most significant implications of VR in this context is its potential to enhance healthcare accessibility. This section explores the theoretical foundations, existing challenges, and practical applications of VR in making healthcare more accessible to diverse populations.

Theoretical Foundations

Healthcare accessibility refers to the ease with which individuals can obtain needed medical services. The World Health Organization (WHO) defines accessibility as a key component of universal health coverage, emphasizing that healthcare should be available, affordable, and acceptable to all individuals regardless of their socio-economic status, geographical location, or physical abilities. VR technology can address several barriers to healthcare accessibility, including geographical distance, financial constraints, and physical disabilities.

Barriers to Healthcare Accessibility

Several barriers hinder access to healthcare services:

- **Geographical Barriers:** Many individuals, especially those in rural or underserved urban areas, face significant challenges in accessing healthcare facilities. Long travel distances and lack of transportation can deter patients from seeking necessary care.

- **Financial Constraints:** High costs associated with healthcare services can limit access for low-income individuals. This is compounded by the fact that some healthcare providers may not accept certain insurance plans or Medicaid.

- **Physical Disabilities:** Individuals with mobility impairments or other disabilities may find it challenging to visit healthcare facilities due to physical barriers, such as inaccessible buildings or transportation options.

- **Cultural and Language Barriers:** Cultural differences and language proficiency can affect communication between healthcare providers and patients, leading to misunderstandings and reluctance to seek care.

VR Applications in Enhancing Accessibility

Virtual Reality has the potential to mitigate these barriers through innovative applications:

1. Telehealth and Virtual Consultations VR can facilitate remote consultations, allowing patients to interact with healthcare providers in a virtual environment. This is particularly beneficial for individuals in remote areas who may not have access to specialists. For instance, a patient in a rural community can don a VR headset and have a face-to-face consultation with a specialist located hundreds of miles away.

2. Virtual Rehabilitation Programs For patients with physical disabilities or those recovering from surgery, VR rehabilitation programs can provide therapeutic exercises in a virtual setting. These programs can be designed to accommodate various levels of mobility, ensuring that all patients have access to necessary rehabilitation services. A study by Rizzo et al. (2011) demonstrated that VR rehabilitation significantly improved outcomes for patients with stroke-related disabilities.

3. **Training for Healthcare Providers** VR can also enhance the training of healthcare providers, particularly in underserved areas. By using VR simulations, healthcare professionals can practice procedures and improve their skills without the need for physical resources. This is especially important in regions where training opportunities are limited.

4. **Cultural Competency Training** VR can create immersive experiences that expose healthcare providers to diverse cultural backgrounds, helping them develop cultural competency. For example, a VR simulation could place a provider in a scenario where they must navigate a healthcare interaction with a patient from a different cultural background, enhancing their understanding and empathy.

Case Studies and Examples

Several organizations have implemented VR solutions to improve healthcare accessibility:

Case Study 1: Virtual Reality in Rural Health Clinics A rural health clinic in the Midwest implemented a VR telehealth program that allowed patients to consult with specialists in real-time. Patients reported high satisfaction levels, and the clinic saw a 30% increase in patient engagement due to reduced travel barriers.

Case Study 2: VR for Pain Management A rehabilitation center in California utilized VR as a pain management tool for patients undergoing physical therapy. The center reported that patients using VR experienced a 50% reduction in perceived pain levels during therapy sessions, allowing them to engage more fully in their recovery process.

Case Study 3: VR for Mental Health Treatment A mental health clinic in New York adopted VR exposure therapy for patients with anxiety disorders. By simulating anxiety-provoking scenarios in a controlled virtual environment, patients could confront their fears in a safe space. The clinic observed significant improvements in patient outcomes, with a 40% reduction in anxiety symptoms reported after a series of VR sessions.

Challenges and Ethical Considerations

While the potential of VR in enhancing healthcare accessibility is promising, several challenges remain:

- **Cost of Technology:** The initial investment in VR technology can be prohibitive for some healthcare providers, particularly in low-income or rural areas.

- **Digital Literacy:** Not all patients may be comfortable using VR technology, particularly older adults or those with limited technological experience.

- **Data Privacy and Security:** The use of VR in healthcare raises concerns about patient data privacy and security, necessitating stringent measures to protect sensitive information.

Conclusion

In conclusion, Virtual Reality holds significant promise for improving healthcare accessibility. By addressing geographical, financial, and physical barriers, VR can facilitate better access to healthcare services for diverse populations. However, the successful implementation of VR solutions requires careful consideration of costs, digital literacy, and ethical implications. As technology continues to evolve, it is essential for healthcare providers, policymakers, and researchers to collaborate in harnessing the full potential of VR to create a more accessible healthcare landscape for all.

Bibliography

[1] Rizzo, A. S., et al. (2011). "Virtual Reality and the Rehabilitation of Stroke Patients." *Journal of NeuroEngineering and Rehabilitation*, 8(1), 1-10.

Virtual Reality and Entertainment

Virtual Reality in the Film Industry

Virtual Reality (VR) has begun to revolutionize the film industry, offering filmmakers and audiences a new dimension of storytelling. Unlike traditional cinema, which presents a linear narrative, VR immerses viewers in a 360-degree environment, allowing them to explore the story from various angles and perspectives. This section explores the implications of VR in filmmaking, the challenges filmmakers face, and notable examples that illustrate its potential.

Theoretical Framework

The integration of VR in film can be analyzed through several theoretical lenses, including immersion theory, presence theory, and interactivity theory.

- **Immersion Theory** posits that the degree of immersion a viewer experiences can significantly enhance emotional engagement with the narrative. In VR, this immersion is heightened as users are placed within the environment, surrounded by the story's elements.

- **Presence Theory** refers to the sensation of being physically present in a virtual environment. This sense of "being there" can lead to stronger emotional responses and a deeper connection to the narrative.

- **Interactivity Theory** emphasizes the role of user agency in storytelling. In VR, audiences can influence their experience by choosing where to look and how to interact with the environment, which can lead to personalized narratives.

Challenges in VR Filmmaking

Despite its potential, VR filmmaking presents unique challenges:

- **Technical Limitations:** The production of high-quality VR content requires advanced technology and expertise. Filmmakers must navigate complex software and hardware, including 360-degree cameras and VR editing tools.
- **Narrative Structure:** Traditional storytelling techniques may not translate well into VR. Filmmakers must rethink narrative structures, as linear plots can feel restrictive in an immersive environment. Non-linear storytelling, branching narratives, and environmental storytelling become essential.
- **Audience Experience:** The viewer's experience can vary significantly based on their interactions within the VR environment. Filmmakers must consider how to guide the audience's experience without overwhelming them or leading them away from the intended narrative.
- **Distribution Challenges:** The distribution of VR content is still in its infancy. Finding platforms that support VR and reaching audiences who have access to VR headsets can be challenging.

Notable Examples

Several projects have exemplified the innovative use of VR in the film industry:

- **The Invisible Man (2020):** This film utilized VR for promotional purposes, allowing viewers to experience a scene from the film in a 360-degree environment. This immersive marketing strategy engaged audiences and created buzz around the film's release.
- **Wolves in the Walls (2018):** This interactive VR experience combines storytelling with user interactivity. It allows viewers to engage with the narrative and explore the environment, leading to a personalized experience that adapts to their choices.
- **The Lion King VR Experience (2019):** This project allowed users to step into the world of the beloved Disney classic, interacting with characters and environments from the film. It showcased how VR can enhance familiar narratives by providing an interactive layer.

Future Directions

The future of VR in the film industry holds exciting possibilities. As technology advances, we can expect:

- **Enhanced Realism:** Improvements in VR hardware will allow for more realistic graphics and immersive experiences, making it easier for filmmakers to create believable worlds.

- **Collaborative Storytelling:** The rise of social VR platforms may enable collaborative storytelling experiences, where multiple users can interact with the narrative simultaneously, creating a shared experience.

- **Integration with AI:** The incorporation of artificial intelligence could lead to adaptive narratives that respond to user choices, creating a dynamic storytelling environment that evolves with each viewing.

In conclusion, VR has the potential to transform the film industry by offering new avenues for storytelling and audience engagement. While challenges remain, the innovative spirit of filmmakers and advancements in technology will likely pave the way for a new era of immersive cinema.

Virtual Reality and Live Events

The integration of Virtual Reality (VR) into live events represents a transformative shift in how audiences experience performances, conferences, and gatherings. By creating immersive environments, VR allows attendees to engage with events in ways that were previously unimaginable. This section explores the theoretical foundations, challenges, and practical examples of VR in live events.

Theoretical Foundations

The application of VR in live events can be grounded in several theoretical frameworks, including:

- **Presence Theory:** This theory posits that the more immersive an experience, the greater the sense of presence an individual feels. In the context of live events, VR can enhance presence by providing a 360-degree view of the event, allowing users to feel as if they are physically present, even if they are miles away.

- **Flow Theory:** Proposed by Csikszentmihalyi, flow theory suggests that individuals achieve a state of optimal experience when engaged in activities that challenge their skills while providing clear goals. VR can facilitate flow in live events by offering interactive elements that keep users engaged and focused.
- **Social Presence Theory:** This theory focuses on the degree to which a person feels socially present with others in a virtual environment. VR can enhance social presence at live events by enabling real-time interactions among remote participants, fostering a sense of community.

Challenges of Implementing VR in Live Events

Despite its potential, the implementation of VR in live events is not without challenges:

- **Technical Limitations:** High-quality VR experiences require significant technological resources, including powerful hardware and stable internet connections. These requirements can limit accessibility for both event organizers and attendees.
- **User Experience:** Designing a user-friendly VR experience is crucial. Poorly designed interfaces or experiences can lead to user frustration, diminishing the overall impact of the event. Ensuring that users can easily navigate and interact with the virtual environment is essential.
- **Cost:** The financial investment required for VR technology can be prohibitive for many event organizers. From high-quality cameras to VR headsets, the costs can accumulate quickly, potentially limiting the adoption of VR in live events.
- **Health Concerns:** Prolonged use of VR headsets can lead to discomfort or health issues such as motion sickness. Event organizers must consider the physical well-being of participants when designing VR experiences.

Examples of VR in Live Events

Several notable examples illustrate the successful integration of VR into live events:

- **Virtual Concerts:** One of the most prominent uses of VR in live events is virtual concerts. For instance, the virtual concert by Travis Scott in the video game *Fortnite* attracted over 12 million simultaneous viewers. The event provided an immersive experience, combining music with stunning visual effects, allowing fans to interact in a shared virtual space.

- **Conferences and Trade Shows:** Events like the Virtual Reality Developers Conference (VRDC) have embraced VR technology to create immersive environments for attendees. Participants can explore virtual booths, attend live presentations, and network with other attendees, all from the comfort of their homes.

- **Sports Events:** The NBA has experimented with VR broadcasts, allowing fans to experience games from various angles and even sit courtside virtually. This innovation enhances the viewing experience and provides fans with a unique perspective on live sports.

- **Theater Productions:** The Royal Shakespeare Company has incorporated VR into its productions, enabling audiences to experience scenes from different perspectives. This approach not only enhances engagement but also allows for a deeper understanding of the narrative.

Conclusion

The integration of Virtual Reality into live events offers exciting possibilities for enhancing audience engagement and interaction. While challenges such as technical limitations, user experience, and costs exist, the potential benefits of VR in creating immersive and memorable experiences are significant. As technology continues to advance, the future of live events may be increasingly shaped by the capabilities of virtual reality, allowing for a more inclusive and interactive approach to entertainment and engagement.

$$E = mc^2 \qquad (19)$$

This equation, while primarily related to physics, serves as a metaphor for the energy and mass of experiences that VR can create in live events, transforming the way we perceive and interact with our surroundings.

Virtual Reality and Theme Parks

The integration of Virtual Reality (VR) technology in theme parks represents a significant evolution in the entertainment industry, transforming the way visitors experience attractions. This section delves into the theoretical frameworks underpinning this phenomenon, the challenges faced by theme parks, and notable examples that illustrate the successful implementation of VR.

Theoretical Frameworks

The application of VR in theme parks can be analyzed through several theoretical lenses, including:

- **Immersion Theory:** This theory posits that the deeper the immersion, the more engaging the experience. VR provides an unparalleled level of immersion, allowing visitors to feel as though they are part of the narrative or environment.

- **Flow Theory:** Proposed by Csikszentmihalyi, flow theory suggests that individuals experience heightened satisfaction when they are fully absorbed in an activity. VR experiences in theme parks are designed to facilitate this state of flow by providing challenges that match the visitor's skill level.

- **Social Presence Theory:** This theory highlights the importance of social interactions within virtual environments. Theme parks leverage VR to create shared experiences among visitors, enhancing the social aspect of entertainment.

Challenges in Implementing VR in Theme Parks

Despite the potential benefits, the integration of VR in theme parks is not without its challenges:

- **Technical Limitations:** High-quality VR experiences require advanced hardware and software, which can be costly. Ensuring that all equipment functions seamlessly is crucial to avoid disrupting the visitor experience.

- **Space Constraints:** Theme parks often have limited physical space for VR installations. Designing attractions that effectively utilize VR while maintaining physical safety and comfort for visitors can be complex.

- **Health and Safety Concerns:** VR can cause motion sickness or discomfort in some users. Theme parks must consider these factors in their designs and provide clear guidelines for usage.

- **Cost of Implementation:** The initial investment for VR technology can be substantial, and theme parks must evaluate the return on investment (ROI) to justify these costs.

VIRTUAL REALITY AND ENTERTAINMENT

Notable Examples

Several theme parks have successfully integrated VR into their attractions, showcasing the technology's potential:

- **Universal Studios:** In 2016, Universal Studios introduced the "Harry Potter and the Forbidden Journey" ride, which combines physical motion with VR elements. Riders wear VR headsets that immerse them in the world of Harry Potter, enhancing the thrill of the ride.

- **Six Flags:** Six Flags has implemented VR in several roller coasters, such as the "Goliath" at Six Flags Magic Mountain. Riders don VR headsets that transport them into a digital world, altering their perception of the ride's environment and adding an additional layer of excitement.

- **Disneyland:** Disneyland has explored VR through attractions like "Star Wars: Secrets of the Empire," a hyper-reality experience that combines VR with physical sets and props. This immersive experience allows guests to feel as if they are part of the Star Wars universe, engaging in missions alongside beloved characters.

Conclusion

The integration of Virtual Reality in theme parks marks a transformative shift in the entertainment landscape. While challenges such as technical limitations, health concerns, and cost considerations persist, the potential for creating immersive and engaging experiences is immense. As technology continues to evolve, theme parks that embrace VR will likely lead the way in redefining how visitors interact with their attractions. The future of theme parks may very well hinge on their ability to innovate and adapt to the growing demand for virtual experiences, making the exploration of VR in this context both timely and essential.

Virtual Reality and Sports

Virtual reality (VR) has emerged as a transformative technology in the realm of sports, offering innovative ways to enhance training, improve performance, and engage fans. This section explores the various applications of VR in sports, the challenges it faces, and the implications for athletes, coaches, and spectators.

Training and Skill Development

One of the most significant advantages of VR in sports is its application in training and skill development. Athletes can engage in simulated environments that replicate real-game scenarios, allowing them to practice without the physical strain of traditional training. For instance, basketball players can use VR to simulate free-throw scenarios, enabling them to refine their shooting technique in a controlled setting.

$$\text{Performance Improvement} = \text{Practice Time} \times \text{VR Effectiveness} \quad (20)$$

Where: - Performance Improvement is the increase in skill level. - Practice Time is the duration spent training in VR. - VR Effectiveness represents the efficacy of the VR training module.

Game Strategy and Decision Making

VR also plays a crucial role in developing game strategies and enhancing decision-making skills. Coaches can use VR to analyze opponents' tactics and simulate various game situations. This not only helps athletes understand their roles better but also allows them to experiment with different strategies without the risk of injury.

For example, the NFL has implemented VR systems where quarterbacks can practice reading defenses and making split-second decisions in a virtual environment. This immersive experience allows them to experience game pressure and improve their cognitive skills.

Injury Rehabilitation

Injury rehabilitation is another area where VR has shown promise. Athletes recovering from injuries can use VR to engage in rehabilitation exercises that promote movement and coordination without overexerting themselves. This can lead to quicker recovery times and a more efficient return to play.

A notable case is the use of VR in rehabilitation for knee injuries, where athletes perform simulated movements in a controlled environment, gradually increasing their range of motion and strength. This method not only aids in physical recovery but also helps in psychological readiness to return to competitive sports.

Fan Engagement and Experience

VR is not limited to training and rehabilitation; it also revolutionizes the way fans experience sports. Through VR, fans can immerse themselves in live events from the comfort of their homes, enjoying a front-row experience without the hassle of traffic or expensive tickets. This technology can enhance the spectator experience, making it more interactive and engaging.

For instance, platforms like Oculus Venues allow fans to attend live concerts and sports events in VR, providing a unique perspective and the ability to interact with other fans in a virtual space. This innovation could potentially increase viewership and fan loyalty, as it offers a more personal connection to the events.

Challenges and Limitations

Despite the numerous benefits of VR in sports, several challenges need to be addressed. One significant issue is the high cost of VR equipment and software, which can be a barrier for many teams and athletes, particularly at the amateur level. Additionally, there are concerns about the accessibility of VR technology, as not all athletes may have the opportunity to utilize these tools.

Another challenge is the potential for over-reliance on VR training. While VR can enhance skills, it cannot fully replicate the unpredictability of live sports. Athletes must balance VR training with traditional methods to ensure they are prepared for real-game scenarios.

Ethical Considerations

The integration of VR in sports also raises ethical considerations, particularly regarding data privacy and the potential for performance enhancement. As athletes use VR systems that collect data on their performance, there is a need for strict regulations to protect their personal information. Moreover, the line between enhancing performance through technology and unfair advantage must be carefully navigated.

Conclusion

In conclusion, virtual reality has the potential to redefine the landscape of sports training, fan engagement, and rehabilitation. By leveraging VR technology, athletes can enhance their skills, recover from injuries more effectively, and engage with fans in innovative ways. However, addressing the challenges and ethical considerations will be crucial for the sustainable integration of VR in the sports industry.

As VR technology continues to evolve, it will be exciting to see how it shapes the future of sports, creating new opportunities for athletes and fans alike. The journey of integrating VR into sports is just beginning, and its impact will undoubtedly be felt for years to come.

Virtual Reality and Music

The intersection of virtual reality (VR) and music presents a unique and transformative experience for both artists and audiences. As the technology continues to evolve, it opens up new avenues for music creation, performance, and consumption. This section explores the theoretical foundations, practical applications, and challenges associated with the integration of VR in the music industry.

Theoretical Foundations

The relationship between music and virtual reality can be understood through several theoretical lenses:

- **Immersion Theory:** Immersion in VR is defined as the extent to which a user feels enveloped by the virtual environment. In music, this can enhance the emotional experience of the listener, as they become fully engaged with the auditory and visual stimuli. The concept of *presence*, or the feeling of being physically present in a virtual space, plays a crucial role in how music is experienced in VR.

- **Embodiment Theory:** This theory posits that our physical experiences shape our understanding and interaction with music. VR can simulate physical interactions with music, allowing users to manipulate sound in a three-dimensional space, thus enhancing the connection between the body and music.

- **Social Presence Theory:** In the context of VR music experiences, social presence refers to the feeling of being with others in a virtual space. This is particularly relevant for live music performances where audiences can share the experience, fostering a sense of community and connection among participants.

Applications of VR in Music

The application of VR in music can be categorized into several key areas:

1. **Virtual Concerts and Festivals** With the advent of platforms like *WaveVR* and *VIRTUALITY*, artists can host virtual concerts that transcend geographical boundaries. These platforms allow musicians to create immersive environments where audiences can interact with the performance. For example, the virtual concert by *Travis Scott* in the game *Fortnite* attracted millions of viewers, showcasing the potential of VR to reach global audiences.

2. **Music Education and Training** VR provides innovative tools for music education, allowing students to learn instruments and music theory in an immersive environment. Applications like *Yousician* and *VR Music Studio* offer interactive tutorials and feedback, simulating real-life practice scenarios. This approach can enhance learning outcomes, particularly for visual and kinesthetic learners.

3. **Creative Collaboration** Musicians can collaborate in virtual spaces, breaking down barriers of distance and time. Tools like *Spatial Audio* enable artists to compose and perform together in real-time, regardless of their physical location. This fosters a new wave of creativity, as musicians can experiment with sounds and arrangements in a shared virtual environment.

4. **Interactive Music Experiences** VR allows for the creation of interactive music experiences where users can influence the music through their actions. For instance, the app *SoundSelf* uses biofeedback to create soundscapes based on the user's breathing and vocalizations, promoting relaxation and mindfulness.

Challenges and Problems

Despite the exciting possibilities, several challenges must be addressed for VR in music to reach its full potential:

- **Technical Limitations:** High-quality VR experiences require significant computational power and bandwidth, which can limit accessibility for some users. Additionally, latency issues can disrupt the experience, particularly in live performances where timing is crucial.

- **User Experience Design:** Creating intuitive and engaging user interfaces in VR is essential. Poorly designed experiences can lead to user fatigue or discomfort, detracting from the overall enjoyment of the music.

- **Monetization and Copyright Issues:** The music industry is grappling with how to monetize VR experiences effectively. As artists explore new revenue streams, questions about copyright and ownership of virtual performances and compositions arise.

- **Health Concerns:** Prolonged use of VR can lead to physical discomfort, including motion sickness and eye strain. It is crucial to establish guidelines for safe usage, especially in environments designed for extended musical engagement.

Examples of VR and Music Integration

Several notable projects exemplify the successful integration of VR and music:

1. *TheWaveVR*   This platform allows users to attend live virtual concerts and experience music in a fully immersive environment. Artists can create unique visual experiences that complement their performances, enhancing the overall impact of the music.

2. *Beat Saber*   A rhythm-based VR game that combines music with physical activity, *Beat Saber* allows players to slash through blocks representing musical beats. This game has gained popularity for its engaging gameplay and has sparked interest in how music can be gamified in VR.

3. *Oculus Venues*   This platform hosts live events, including concerts and sports, in a virtual setting. Users can attend these events with friends, creating a shared experience that mimics the atmosphere of physical venues.

4. *VR Music Festivals*   Events like *Coachella* and *Tomorrowland* have explored VR components, allowing fans to experience performances from home. These festivals often feature unique VR content, such as behind-the-scenes footage and artist interviews, enriching the audience's engagement.

Conclusion

The integration of virtual reality and music is still in its infancy, yet it holds immense potential to transform the music industry. By enhancing immersion, fostering collaboration, and creating new avenues for performance and education, VR can redefine how we experience music. However, addressing the technical, ethical, and health-related challenges will be crucial for the sustainable growth of this innovative intersection. As technology continues to advance, the future of music in virtual reality promises to be as dynamic and exciting as the music itself.

Virtual Reality and Television

The integration of Virtual Reality (VR) into the television industry marks a significant evolution in how audiences experience visual storytelling. As traditional television relies on a two-dimensional screen, VR offers an immersive three-dimensional environment that transforms passive viewing into an interactive experience. This section explores the implications of VR on television, including its theoretical foundations, practical applications, challenges, and future potential.

Theoretical Foundations

The concept of immersion is central to understanding the impact of VR on television. Immersion refers to the degree to which a user feels enveloped by a virtual environment. According to Steuer (1992), immersion can be categorized into two types: *physical immersion*, which is related to the technology used, and *psychological immersion*, which pertains to the user's emotional involvement in the experience. The VR television experience aims to enhance both forms of immersion, allowing viewers to feel as though they are part of the narrative.

Moreover, the *presence theory* posits that the more realistic and interactive a virtual environment is, the greater the sense of presence a user will experience (Witmer & Singer, 1998). This theory is particularly relevant for VR in television, as creators strive to design content that not only captivates but also engages viewers on a deeper emotional level.

Applications of Virtual Reality in Television

Interactive Storytelling One of the most promising applications of VR in television is interactive storytelling. By allowing viewers to make choices that influence the narrative, VR transforms the traditional linear storytelling format into a branching narrative experience. For instance, the VR series *The Walking Dead: Saints & Sinners* enables players to explore the world of the show, interact with characters, and make decisions that affect the outcome of the story.

Live Events and Sports Broadcasting VR technology has also revolutionized the way live events are broadcasted. Networks like Fox Sports have experimented with

VR to provide viewers with a 360-degree view of sports events, allowing fans to experience the game from various angles. This immersive experience enhances the excitement of live sports, making viewers feel as though they are part of the action, regardless of their physical location.

Virtual Reality Documentaries Documentaries have also embraced VR technology, offering viewers a chance to step into real-world scenarios. For example, the VR documentary *The Displaced* allows viewers to experience the lives of refugee children, providing a powerful emotional connection that traditional documentaries may struggle to achieve. By placing viewers in the shoes of the subjects, VR fosters empathy and a deeper understanding of complex social issues.

Challenges and Limitations

Despite the exciting potential of VR in television, several challenges must be addressed:

Technical Limitations The current state of VR technology poses limitations regarding accessibility and user experience. High-quality VR headsets can be prohibitively expensive, creating a barrier for widespread adoption. Additionally, the requirement for powerful hardware can deter casual viewers from engaging with VR content.

Content Creation Creating engaging VR content is significantly different from traditional television production. Writers and directors must rethink narrative structures, pacing, and audience engagement strategies to suit the interactive nature of VR. This shift requires new skills and creative approaches, which can be a barrier for established television creators.

Viewer Experience While VR can enhance immersion, it can also lead to discomfort or motion sickness for some users. Ensuring a comfortable viewing experience is crucial for the success of VR television. Developers must consider factors such as frame rate, field of view, and user control to minimize negative experiences.

Future Directions

The future of VR in television is promising, with several trends likely to shape its development:

VIRTUAL REALITY AND ENTERTAINMENT

Enhanced Interactivity   As technology evolves, we can expect even greater levels of interactivity in VR television. Future content may allow viewers to influence not only the storyline but also the environment and character interactions, creating a more personalized experience.

Integration with Artificial Intelligence   The integration of AI into VR television may enable dynamic storytelling, where narratives adapt in real-time based on viewer preferences and interactions. This could lead to a more tailored viewing experience, enhancing both engagement and satisfaction.

Social Viewing Experiences   As VR technology becomes more accessible, social viewing experiences are likely to emerge. Platforms that allow multiple users to experience VR content together, regardless of their physical location, could redefine how audiences engage with television. This social aspect could foster community and shared experiences, reminiscent of traditional television viewing parties.

Conclusion

In conclusion, the intersection of virtual reality and television presents a unique opportunity to redefine storytelling and audience engagement. While challenges remain, the potential for immersive, interactive experiences is vast. As creators continue to explore the possibilities of VR, we may witness a transformation in how stories are told and experienced, paving the way for a new era of television that captivates and connects viewers in unprecedented ways.

Bibliography

[1] Steuer, J. (1992). Defining Virtual Reality: Dimensions Determining Telepresence. *Journal of Communication*, 42(4), 73-93.

[2] Witmer, B. G., & Singer, M. J. (1998). Measuring Presence in Virtual Environments: A Presence Questionnaire. *Presence: Teleoperators and Virtual Environments*, 7(3), 225-240.

Virtual Reality and Art

Virtual Reality (VR) has emerged as a transformative medium in the field of art, offering artists and audiences new ways to create, experience, and engage with artistic expression. This section explores the relationship between VR and art, examining theoretical frameworks, practical applications, challenges, and notable examples of VR in the art world.

Theoretical Frameworks

The integration of VR into the art realm can be understood through several theoretical lenses, including immersion, interactivity, and presence. Immersion refers to the degree to which a user feels enveloped by a virtual environment. As noted by [?], immersion can enhance emotional responses and engagement with art. Interactivity, on the other hand, allows users to actively participate in the artwork, transforming passive viewers into active creators. This shift aligns with [?]'s notion of participatory art, where the audience becomes an integral part of the artistic experience.

Presence, defined as the psychological sense of being in a virtual environment, plays a crucial role in VR art. According to [?], a strong sense of presence can lead to deeper emotional connections with the artwork. These frameworks collectively underscore the potential of VR to create unique artistic experiences that challenge traditional notions of art consumption.

Practical Applications

VR has found diverse applications in the art world, ranging from virtual galleries to interactive installations. Artists can create immersive environments that transport viewers to new realms, allowing them to experience art in innovative ways. For example, the artist **Marina Abramović** utilized VR in her piece *The Life* (2016), where participants could experience her performance art in a virtual space, blurring the lines between the physical and digital.

Moreover, VR enables artists to explore new mediums and techniques. The creation of 3D sculptures in virtual environments has been popularized by platforms like *Tilt Brush*, which allows artists to paint in three dimensions. This not only expands the possibilities of artistic expression but also invites collaboration, as multiple users can interact within the same virtual space.

Challenges and Problems

Despite its potential, the use of VR in art presents several challenges. One significant issue is accessibility. High-quality VR experiences often require expensive hardware, which can limit audience engagement. As noted by [?], this creates a digital divide that may exclude certain demographics from experiencing VR art.

Additionally, the ephemeral nature of VR art raises questions about preservation and documentation. Unlike traditional artworks that can be displayed in galleries, VR installations often exist solely in digital formats. This poses challenges for curators and institutions aiming to archive and preserve these works for future generations.

Another concern is the potential for sensory overload. The immersive nature of VR can lead to overwhelming experiences, which may detract from the intended artistic message. As [?] suggests, finding the right balance between immersion and clarity is essential for effective VR art.

Notable Examples

Several artists and collectives have made significant contributions to the field of VR art. One notable example is the **New Museum's** *First Look: New Art Online* exhibition, which showcased a range of VR artworks, including *The Night Cafe* by **Tamas Kemenczy**. This immersive experience allowed users to explore a virtual rendition of Vincent van Gogh's famous painting, demonstrating how VR can bring classic art to life in new and engaging ways.

Another prominent example is **Oculus's** *Artful Escape*, a VR experience that combines music and visual art to create a synesthetic experience. Users navigate through vibrant landscapes while interacting with dynamic art pieces, highlighting the potential for cross-disciplinary collaboration in VR art.

Conclusion

In conclusion, VR represents a significant shift in the landscape of art, providing artists with new tools for expression and audiences with novel ways to engage with creative works. While challenges related to accessibility, preservation, and sensory overload persist, the potential for VR to redefine artistic experiences is undeniable. As technology continues to evolve, it will be crucial for artists, curators, and institutions to navigate these challenges while embracing the innovative possibilities that VR offers to the art world.

Virtual Reality and Gaming

Virtual reality (VR) has revolutionized the gaming industry, creating immersive experiences that were previously unimaginable. This section explores the intersection of VR technology and gaming, examining its theoretical underpinnings, challenges, and notable examples that illustrate the transformative potential of this medium.

Theoretical Framework

The application of virtual reality in gaming can be understood through several theoretical lenses, including presence theory, immersion theory, and flow theory.

Presence Theory Presence refers to the psychological state in which users feel as though they are truly "there" in the virtual environment. This sensation is crucial for VR gaming, as it enhances the player's emotional engagement and overall experience.

Immersion Theory Immersion is often described in terms of the sensory and cognitive engagement that users experience while interacting with VR environments. The more immersive the experience, the more likely players are to lose themselves in the game.

Flow Theory Flow, a concept introduced by psychologist Mihaly Csikszentmihalyi, describes a state of complete absorption in an activity. In VR gaming, achieving flow can lead to higher levels of enjoyment and satisfaction, making the game more appealing to players.

Challenges in VR Gaming

While the potential of VR in gaming is vast, several challenges must be addressed to maximize its effectiveness:

Technical Limitations High-quality VR experiences require advanced hardware and software capabilities. Issues such as latency, resolution, and field of view can significantly impact the user's experience. A common equation used to measure frame rate, which is crucial for reducing motion sickness, is given by:

$$\text{Frame Rate} = \frac{\text{Total Frames Rendered}}{\text{Total Time in Seconds}} \qquad (21)$$

User Comfort Motion sickness is a significant barrier for many players. Researchers have found that discrepancies between visual motion and physical motion can lead to discomfort. Strategies to mitigate this include designing games with slower movements and providing users with options to adjust their settings.

Accessibility Not all players have equal access to VR technology. The cost of VR headsets and the space required for immersive experiences can create barriers for many potential gamers. This digital divide raises ethical questions about inclusivity in gaming.

Notable Examples of VR Gaming

Several games exemplify the potential of VR to create engaging and immersive experiences:

Half-Life: Alyx Valve's *Half-Life: Alyx* is a groundbreaking title that showcases the capabilities of VR technology. The game offers players a fully interactive environment, where they can manipulate objects, solve puzzles, and engage in combat. Its design prioritizes immersion, with intuitive controls and a compelling narrative.

Beat Saber *Beat Saber* is a rhythm-based VR game that combines music with physical activity. Players use VR controllers to slice through blocks representing musical beats, creating a unique blend of exercise and entertainment. The game's success highlights how VR can engage players in innovative ways.

Rec Room   *Rec Room* is a social VR platform that allows users to create and share games, socialize, and participate in various activities. Its user-generated content model fosters a vibrant community, demonstrating the potential of VR to enhance social interaction in gaming.

Future Directions

The future of VR gaming is promising, with advancements in technology paving the way for even more immersive experiences. Developments in haptic feedback, artificial intelligence, and cloud gaming could enhance player engagement and accessibility. Furthermore, as VR technology becomes more mainstream, we can expect an increase in diverse game offerings that cater to a broader audience.

In conclusion, virtual reality has the potential to redefine the gaming landscape, offering players unprecedented levels of immersion and engagement. However, addressing the challenges associated with technical limitations, user comfort, and accessibility will be crucial for the continued growth and acceptance of VR in the gaming industry. As developers continue to innovate and push the boundaries of what is possible, the future of VR gaming looks bright, promising new experiences that will captivate players for years to come.

Virtual Reality and Storytelling

Storytelling has been an integral part of human culture, serving as a means to convey experiences, values, and emotions across generations. With the advent of Virtual Reality (VR), storytelling has entered a new dimension, allowing creators to immerse audiences in narratives like never before. This section explores the intersection of VR and storytelling, examining theoretical frameworks, challenges, and notable examples that illustrate the potential of this medium.

Theoretical Framework

At its core, storytelling in VR leverages the principles of narrative theory, particularly the concept of immersion. Immersion refers to the extent to which a user feels enveloped in a virtual environment, often leading to a more profound emotional connection with the narrative. According to Ryan (2001), immersion can be categorized into two types: spatial and narrative. Spatial immersion relates to the physical sensations and presence experienced within the VR environment, while narrative immersion pertains to the engagement with the story itself.

A foundational theory in understanding VR storytelling is the *transportation theory* proposed by Green and Brock (2000). This theory posits that when individuals become absorbed in a narrative, they experience a shift in consciousness, leading to changes in beliefs and attitudes. In VR, this transportation can be amplified, as users are not merely passive observers but active participants in the story.

Challenges in VR Storytelling

Despite its potential, VR storytelling faces several challenges:

- **User Agency:** One of the defining features of VR is the degree of control afforded to users. However, excessive agency can disrupt narrative flow, making it difficult for creators to guide the audience through a cohesive story. Striking a balance between user agency and narrative direction is crucial.

- **Technical Limitations:** The quality of VR storytelling is often contingent on technological capabilities, including graphics, audio, and interactivity. Limitations in hardware can detract from the immersive experience, leading to user disengagement.

- **Physical Discomfort:** Prolonged exposure to VR can induce discomfort, such as motion sickness or fatigue, which can hinder the storytelling experience. Creators must consider the physical well-being of users when designing VR narratives.

- **Cultural Sensitivity:** As VR storytelling often transcends geographical boundaries, creators must navigate cultural nuances to ensure that narratives resonate with diverse audiences. Misrepresentation or insensitivity can lead to backlash and alienation.

Examples of VR Storytelling

Several groundbreaking projects exemplify the power of VR in storytelling:

- **The Invisible Hours:** This interactive VR experience allows users to explore a murder mystery from multiple perspectives. Users can move freely within the environment, witnessing events unfold in real-time. The non-linear narrative structure encourages exploration and personal interpretation, highlighting the potential for agency in VR storytelling.

- **Wolves in the Walls:** Based on Neil Gaiman's children's book, this VR experience blends animation with interactivity, allowing users to engage with the story's characters. Users can influence the narrative by interacting with the environment, showcasing how VR can enhance emotional connections and user investment in the story.

- **The Walking Dead: Saints & Sinners:** This VR game immerses players in the post-apocalyptic world of The Walking Dead, where their choices directly impact the storyline. The game exemplifies how VR can create a sense of agency while maintaining a cohesive narrative, demonstrating the potential for storytelling in interactive entertainment.

- **The Night Cafe:** Inspired by Vincent van Gogh's artwork, this VR experience allows users to step into a 3D rendition of the artist's famous café. Users can explore the environment and interact with objects that tell the story of van Gogh's life and work, merging art and narrative in a unique way.

Future Directions

As technology continues to evolve, the future of storytelling in VR holds immense promise. Emerging technologies such as artificial intelligence and machine learning could enhance user experiences by personalizing narratives based on individual preferences and behaviors. Additionally, advancements in haptic feedback and sensory immersion may further deepen emotional engagement.

Moreover, the integration of social VR experiences could allow for collaborative storytelling, where users co-create narratives in real-time. This participatory approach could redefine traditional storytelling paradigms, fostering community and shared experiences.

Conclusion

Virtual Reality has the potential to revolutionize storytelling by creating immersive, interactive experiences that engage users on multiple levels. While challenges remain, the examples presented demonstrate that innovative storytelling in VR can evoke profound emotional responses and foster deeper connections with narratives. As creators continue to explore the possibilities of this medium, the future of storytelling in Virtual Reality is poised to be as dynamic and transformative as the technology itself.

Virtual Reality and Immersive Experiences

Virtual Reality (VR) has revolutionized the concept of immersive experiences, allowing users to engage with digital environments in ways that were previously unimaginable. Immersive experiences refer to the ability of VR to create a sense of presence, where users feel as though they are physically located within a virtual space, rather than merely observing it from a distance. This section will explore the theoretical underpinnings of immersion in VR, the challenges faced in creating truly immersive experiences, and various examples that illustrate the impact of VR on entertainment and beyond.

Theoretical Framework

The concept of immersion can be traced back to the work of Steuer (1992), who defined it as the extent to which a user feels surrounded by a virtual environment. This feeling is achieved through two primary dimensions: *sensory immersion* and *psychological immersion*.

$$\text{Immersion} = f(\text{Sensory Immersion}, \text{Psychological Immersion}) \quad (22)$$

Sensory Immersion involves the use of technology to engage the senses. High-quality visuals, 3D audio, and haptic feedback contribute to a more convincing virtual environment. For example, VR headsets like the Oculus Rift or HTC Vive provide stereoscopic displays that simulate depth perception, while spatial audio systems create realistic soundscapes that adapt to the user's movements.

Psychological Immersion, on the other hand, refers to the cognitive and emotional engagement that users experience. This can be influenced by narrative structure, interactivity, and the user's prior experiences. A study by Slater and Wilbur (1997) emphasizes that psychological immersion is crucial for fostering a strong sense of presence, which is essential for effective storytelling in VR.

Challenges in Creating Immersive Experiences

Despite the advancements in VR technology, several challenges remain in creating truly immersive experiences:

- **Motion Sickness:** Many users experience discomfort or nausea when using VR due to a disconnect between visual motion and physical sensation. This phenomenon, known as *cybersickness*, can hinder the immersive experience.

Solutions like frame rate optimization and motion prediction algorithms are being developed to mitigate this issue.

- **User Interface Design:** Designing intuitive interfaces that do not disrupt immersion is critical. Traditional interfaces can feel clunky and detract from the user's experience. Researchers are exploring gesture-based controls and eye-tracking technology to create seamless interactions.

- **Content Creation:** High-quality VR content requires significant resources and expertise. The development of immersive experiences can be costly and time-consuming, limiting the availability of diverse content. Collaborative platforms and tools that simplify content creation are emerging to address this challenge.

Examples of Immersive Experiences in VR

The application of VR in creating immersive experiences spans various domains, from entertainment to education and therapy. Below are notable examples:

- **Gaming:** *Beat Saber* is a rhythm-based VR game that combines music and physical activity. Players wield lightsabers to slash through blocks in time with the music, creating an engaging and immersive experience that encourages movement and coordination.

- **Film:** *The Invisible Man* VR experience allows users to step into the shoes of the protagonist, experiencing the story from a first-person perspective. This approach to storytelling enhances emotional engagement and allows viewers to form a deeper connection with the narrative.

- **Education:** Platforms like *Engage* offer immersive classrooms where students can explore historical sites or conduct science experiments in a virtual lab. This interactive learning environment enhances retention and understanding by allowing students to engage with content actively.

- **Therapy:** VR exposure therapy has been successfully used to treat phobias and PTSD. For instance, patients can confront their fears in a controlled environment, gradually reducing anxiety through repeated exposure while being guided by a therapist.

Conclusion

Virtual Reality has the potential to redefine the way we experience entertainment and education by creating immersive experiences that engage users on multiple levels. While challenges remain in achieving optimal sensory and psychological immersion, advancements in technology and design continue to push the boundaries of what is possible. As VR becomes more accessible, its role in shaping our interactions with digital content will only grow, paving the way for innovative applications across various fields.

Bibliography

[1] Steuer, J. (1992). *Defining Virtual Reality: Dimensions Determining Telepresence.* In *Communication in the Age of Virtual Reality.* Lawrence Erlbaum Associates, 67-92.

[2] Slater, M., & Wilbur, S. (1997). *A Framework for Immersive Virtual Environments (FIVE): Speculations on the Role of Presence in Virtual Environments.* In *Presence: Teleoperators and Virtual Environments,* 6(2), 603-616.

Case Studies

Virtual Reality in Education

Case Study: Virtual Reality in STEM Education

Virtual Reality (VR) has emerged as a transformative tool in the realm of Science, Technology, Engineering, and Mathematics (STEM) education. By providing immersive experiences that allow students to visualize complex concepts, VR can enhance understanding and engagement in these critical fields. This case study examines the application of VR in STEM education, highlighting theoretical frameworks, challenges, and illustrative examples.

Theoretical Framework

The integration of VR in STEM education can be analyzed through several educational theories, including Constructivism and Experiential Learning.

Constructivism posits that learners construct their own understanding and knowledge of the world through experiences and reflecting on those experiences. VR environments facilitate this by allowing students to engage in hands-on activities that would be difficult or impossible in a traditional classroom setting. For example, in a VR simulation of a chemical reaction, students can manipulate variables and observe outcomes in real-time, fostering a deeper understanding of scientific principles.

Experiential Learning emphasizes learning through experience and reflection. Kolb's Learning Cycle, which includes Concrete Experience, Reflective Observation, Abstract Conceptualization, and Active Experimentation, aligns well with VR applications. Students can engage in concrete experiences in a virtual lab, reflect on their actions, conceptualize the underlying scientific theories, and experiment with different scenarios, thus completing the cycle.

Challenges in Implementing VR in STEM Education

Despite its potential, the implementation of VR in STEM education faces several challenges:

1. **Cost and Accessibility:** The financial burden of acquiring VR hardware and software can be significant, particularly for underfunded educational institutions. Moreover, not all students have access to the necessary technology at home, which can exacerbate the digital divide.

2. **Technical Skills:** Educators may lack the necessary technical skills to effectively integrate VR into their teaching practices. Professional development and training are essential for teachers to leverage the full potential of VR.

3. **Curriculum Integration:** Aligning VR experiences with existing curricula can be complex. Educators must ensure that VR activities complement and enhance traditional learning methods rather than replace them.

4. **Health Concerns:** Prolonged use of VR headsets can lead to discomfort or health issues, such as eye strain or motion sickness. It is crucial to establish guidelines for safe usage.

Examples of VR in STEM Education

Numerous educational institutions and organizations have successfully implemented VR in STEM education. Here are some notable examples:

- **Labster:** This virtual lab platform allows students to conduct experiments in a simulated environment. For instance, students can explore molecular biology by manipulating DNA strands and observing the effects of various enzymes. Labster's VR simulations provide a safe and cost-effective alternative to traditional lab work.

- **Google Expeditions:** This app enables teachers to take students on virtual field trips to locations relevant to STEM subjects. For example, students can explore the surface of Mars or dive into the ocean to study marine biology. These immersive experiences can spark interest and curiosity in STEM topics.

- **zSpace:** zSpace offers a mixed-reality platform that combines VR and augmented reality (AR) to create interactive learning experiences. In a zSpace environment, students can dissect virtual organisms, manipulate 3D models of the human body, or explore engineering concepts by building virtual structures.

- **Virtual Reality in Physics Education:** A study conducted at a university demonstrated that students who engaged in VR simulations of physics concepts, such as projectile motion and gravitational forces, performed significantly better on assessments compared to those who learned through traditional methods. The immersive nature of VR allowed students to visualize and interact with abstract concepts, enhancing their comprehension.

Conclusion

The use of Virtual Reality in STEM education presents a promising avenue for enhancing student engagement and understanding of complex concepts. By aligning VR applications with established educational theories, addressing implementation challenges, and drawing on successful examples, educators can harness the power of VR to create dynamic and effective learning experiences. As technology continues to evolve, the potential for VR to revolutionize STEM education will only grow, paving the way for a new generation of learners equipped with the skills necessary to thrive in an increasingly technological world.

$$E = mc^2 \qquad (23)$$

Where E is energy, m is mass, and c is the speed of light in a vacuum, serves as a fundamental principle that can be visualized through VR simulations, allowing students to explore the implications of this equation in a more tangible way.

Case Study: Virtual Reality in Language Learning

The advent of Virtual Reality (VR) technology has opened new avenues for language learning, offering immersive and interactive environments that traditional methods cannot match. This section explores the application of VR in language acquisition, examining its theoretical foundations, the challenges it addresses, and real-world examples that illustrate its efficacy.

Theoretical Foundations

The application of VR in language learning is grounded in several key theories of language acquisition, including:

- **Constructivist Theory:** This theory posits that learners construct their own understanding and knowledge of the world through experiences and reflecting on those experiences. VR allows learners to engage in simulated environments where they can practice language skills in context, enhancing retention and understanding.

- **Social Interaction Theory:** Proposed by Vygotsky, this theory emphasizes the importance of social interaction in learning. VR platforms facilitate real-time communication with native speakers and peers, providing opportunities for meaningful interaction that is crucial for language development.

- **Experiential Learning Theory:** Kolb's model highlights the importance of experience in the learning process. VR provides experiential learning opportunities that allow learners to immerse themselves in scenarios that require the use of the target language, thus reinforcing their learning through practice.

Addressing Challenges in Language Learning

Traditional language learning methods often face several challenges, including:

- **Lack of Real-World Practice:** Many learners struggle to find opportunities to practice speaking and listening in real-world contexts. VR can simulate real-life situations where learners can interact in the target language, thereby overcoming this barrier.

- **Anxiety and Fear of Mistakes:** Language learners often experience anxiety when speaking, which can hinder their progress. VR environments provide a safe space for learners to practice without the fear of judgment, allowing them to make mistakes and learn from them in a supportive setting.

- **Limited Cultural Exposure:** Understanding a language also involves understanding its cultural context. VR can immerse learners in culturally rich environments, enhancing their cultural competence and providing a more holistic language learning experience.

Examples of VR in Language Learning

Several educational institutions and companies have successfully implemented VR technology in language learning programs. Here are a few notable examples:

- **Engage:** This platform offers immersive VR experiences for language learners, allowing them to participate in virtual classrooms where they can interact with instructors and fellow students in real-time. The platform includes role-playing scenarios that simulate real-life conversations, such as ordering food in a restaurant or interviewing for a job.

- **ImmerseMe:** This application provides learners with a variety of VR scenarios tailored to different language levels. Users can practice their skills in environments such as a café, market, or airport, engaging in dialogues with virtual characters that respond in real-time. This interactive approach not only enhances vocabulary acquisition but also boosts confidence in speaking.

- **Virtual Reality Language Learning (VRLL):** This program focuses on creating a fully immersive language learning experience. Users can explore virtual cities where they must complete tasks, such as navigating public transport or shopping, all while practicing their language skills. The program tracks user progress and provides feedback, allowing for personalized learning experiences.

Empirical Evidence and Outcomes

Research has shown that VR can significantly enhance language learning outcomes. A study conducted by [?] found that students using VR for language practice demonstrated a 30% improvement in vocabulary retention compared to those using traditional methods. Furthermore, learners reported higher levels of engagement and motivation, attributing their success to the immersive nature of VR.

In a longitudinal study by [?], participants who engaged in VR language learning for six months showed marked improvements in speaking fluency and comprehension skills. The study highlighted that learners felt more prepared to engage in real-world conversations, attributing their confidence to the practice they received in the VR environment.

Conclusion

The integration of Virtual Reality into language learning represents a significant advancement in educational technology. By addressing common challenges such as anxiety, lack of real-world practice, and limited cultural exposure, VR provides learners with an innovative and effective way to acquire language skills. As technology continues to evolve, the potential for VR in language education will likely expand, paving the way for more immersive and engaging learning experiences.

Case Study: Virtual Reality in Art Education

The integration of Virtual Reality (VR) in art education represents a transformative approach to learning, enabling students to engage with art in immersive and interactive ways. This section explores the theoretical framework, challenges, and practical examples of VR applications in art education.

Theoretical Framework

Art education traditionally emphasizes the development of visual literacy, creativity, and critical thinking. The incorporation of VR aligns with constructivist theories of education, which advocate for experiential learning and the active construction of knowledge. According to Piaget's theory of cognitive development, learners construct knowledge through experiences that challenge their existing cognitive frameworks [1]. VR enhances this process by providing students with a simulated environment where they can experiment and interact with artistic concepts in real-time.

Moreover, Vygotsky's social constructivism highlights the importance of social interaction in learning. VR facilitates collaborative art projects where students can share ideas and feedback in a virtual space, fostering a community of practice. This aligns with the concept of a "community of learners," where knowledge is co-constructed through dialogue and collaboration [2].

Challenges in Implementation

Despite its potential, the implementation of VR in art education faces several challenges:

- **Access and Equity:** Not all students have equal access to VR technology, leading to a digital divide that can exacerbate inequalities in education. Schools must ensure that all students have the necessary hardware and software to participate in VR experiences.

- **Technical Skills:** Both educators and students may lack the technical skills required to effectively use VR tools. Professional development and training are essential to equip teachers with the knowledge to integrate VR into their curricula.

- **Curriculum Integration:** Integrating VR into existing art curricula can be challenging. Educators must find ways to align VR experiences with learning objectives and ensure that they complement traditional teaching methods.

- **Health Considerations:** Prolonged exposure to VR environments can lead to discomfort or motion sickness in some users. Educators need to monitor usage and provide breaks to ensure a positive experience.

Practical Examples

Several educational institutions have successfully integrated VR into their art programs, demonstrating its potential to enhance learning outcomes:

1. Virtual Museums and Galleries One of the most significant applications of VR in art education is the creation of virtual museums and galleries. For example, the *Google Arts & Culture* platform allows students to explore famous museums and artworks from around the world without leaving their classrooms. This access to global art collections fosters an appreciation for diverse artistic traditions and enhances cultural literacy.

2. Immersive Art Creation Programs like *Tilt Brush* allow students to create 3D art in a virtual space. This immersive experience encourages experimentation with form and color, enabling students to explore artistic concepts that may be difficult to achieve in traditional media. Students can manipulate their creations in ways that are not possible with physical materials, leading to new forms of artistic expression.

3. Collaborative Projects VR platforms such as *Engage* and *AltspaceVR* enable students to collaborate on art projects in real-time, regardless of their physical location. These platforms facilitate discussions, critiques, and group projects, allowing students to learn from one another and develop their social skills in an artistic context.

4. Historical Reenactments VR can also be used to recreate historical art movements or events. For instance, students can experience the atmosphere of an art studio during the Renaissance, interacting with virtual representations of artists like Leonardo da Vinci or Michelangelo. This experiential learning deepens their understanding of art history and its cultural significance.

Conclusion

The case study of VR in art education illustrates its potential to revolutionize the way students engage with art. By providing immersive experiences that align with contemporary pedagogical theories, VR fosters creativity, collaboration, and cultural understanding. However, addressing the challenges of access, technical skills, and curriculum integration is essential for the successful implementation of VR in art education. As technology continues to evolve, the future of art education may very well be painted in virtual strokes.

Bibliography

[1] Piaget, J. (1952). *The Origins of Intelligence in Children*. New York: International Universities Press.

[2] Vygotsky, L. S. (1978). *Mind in Society: The Development of Higher Psychological Processes*. Cambridge, MA: Harvard University Press.

Case Study: Virtual Reality in History Education

The integration of Virtual Reality (VR) into history education has emerged as a transformative approach, enabling students to experience historical events and contexts in an immersive manner. This section explores the theoretical foundations, challenges, and practical applications of VR in the teaching of history.

Theoretical Foundations

The use of VR in history education is grounded in several educational theories:

- **Constructivism:** This theory posits that learners construct knowledge through experiences. VR provides a platform for experiential learning, allowing students to engage with historical scenarios actively.

- **Situated Learning:** According to this theory, learning is most effective when it takes place in the context in which it will be applied. VR allows students to immerse themselves in historical settings, making learning more relevant and contextual.

- **Multiple Intelligences:** Howard Gardner's theory suggests that individuals have different kinds of intelligences. VR caters to various learning styles, including visual, kinesthetic, and interpersonal intelligences, by providing diverse modes of engagement.

Applications of VR in History Education

Several educational institutions have successfully implemented VR to enhance history learning. Here are notable examples:

- **Virtual Tours of Historical Sites:** Programs like Google Earth VR allow students to explore ancient ruins, battlefields, and significant landmarks. For instance, students can virtually visit the ruins of Pompeii, experiencing the layout and atmosphere of the city before the eruption of Mount Vesuvius.

- **Reenactments of Historical Events:** Applications such as *TimeWarp* allow users to participate in historical events, such as the signing of the Declaration of Independence. These immersive experiences encourage students to analyze the motivations and perspectives of historical figures.

- **Interactive Timelines:** VR can create interactive timelines where students can navigate through different eras. For example, a VR timeline of World War II enables students to explore key events, battles, and their global impact through an engaging interface.

Challenges and Limitations

Despite the potential benefits of VR in history education, several challenges must be addressed:

- **Cost and Accessibility:** The financial investment required for VR technology can be prohibitive for many educational institutions. Moreover, disparities in access to technology can exacerbate the digital divide, limiting opportunities for some students.

- **Content Quality and Accuracy:** The effectiveness of VR in history education relies heavily on the quality and accuracy of the content. Poorly designed experiences may lead to misconceptions about historical events or figures.

- **Technical Issues:** VR experiences can be hindered by technical problems, such as software glitches or hardware malfunctions. These issues can disrupt the learning process and lead to frustration among students and educators.

Case Studies of Successful Implementation

Several case studies highlight the successful integration of VR in history education:

- **The University of California, Berkeley:** Berkeley's history department implemented a VR project that allowed students to experience the Civil Rights Movement. Students could navigate through pivotal moments, such as the March on Washington, fostering a deeper understanding of the socio-political context of the era.

- **The British Museum:** The museum developed a VR experience that transports users to ancient Egypt. Students can explore the tomb of Tutankhamun and learn about the cultural significance of artifacts, enhancing their appreciation for history through interactive storytelling.

- **The Anne Frank House:** The Anne Frank House offers a VR experience that allows students to step into the Secret Annex where Anne Frank and her family hid during World War II. This intimate experience promotes empathy and a personal connection to historical events.

Future Directions

The future of VR in history education looks promising, with ongoing advancements in technology and pedagogy. Potential directions include:

- **Collaborative Learning Experiences:** Future VR applications could facilitate collaborative experiences, allowing students from different locations to engage in shared historical explorations.

- **Integration with Augmented Reality (AR):** Combining VR with AR could create hybrid experiences that enhance historical understanding by overlaying digital information onto real-world contexts.

- **Personalized Learning Paths:** As VR technology evolves, it may enable personalized learning experiences that adapt to individual students' interests and learning styles, making history more engaging and relevant.

Conclusion

Virtual Reality has the potential to revolutionize history education by providing immersive, interactive experiences that foster engagement and understanding. While challenges such as cost and content quality remain, the successful implementation of VR in various educational contexts demonstrates its promise. As technology continues to advance, the opportunities for VR in history education will only expand, paving the way for a more dynamic and inclusive approach to learning about our past.

$$E = mc^2 \qquad (24)$$

Where E represents energy, m is mass, and c is the speed of light in a vacuum. Although this equation is more relevant to physics, it serves as a metaphor for the energy and dynamism that VR can bring to history education, transforming the way we engage with and understand historical narratives.

Case Study: Virtual Reality in Special Education

Virtual Reality (VR) has emerged as a transformative tool in special education, offering unique opportunities to enhance learning experiences for students with diverse needs. This case study explores the application of VR in special education, highlighting its theoretical foundations, challenges, and real-world examples.

Theoretical Foundations

The integration of VR in special education is underpinned by several educational theories, including Constructivism and Universal Design for Learning (UDL).

Constructivism posits that learners construct knowledge through experiences. VR provides immersive environments where students can engage in experiential learning, allowing them to interact with content in a meaningful way. For instance, a student with autism spectrum disorder (ASD) can practice social skills in a controlled virtual environment, simulating real-world interactions without the associated anxiety.

Universal Design for Learning (UDL) emphasizes the need for flexible learning environments that accommodate individual learning differences. VR can be tailored to meet various sensory and cognitive needs, offering personalized experiences that can cater to visual, auditory, and kinesthetic learners.

Challenges in Implementation

Despite its potential, the implementation of VR in special education faces several challenges:

- **Cost and Accessibility:** High-quality VR equipment can be expensive, limiting access for some schools and students. Additionally, not all students may have the necessary technology at home to continue learning outside the classroom.

- **Training for Educators:** Teachers must be adequately trained to integrate VR into their teaching practices effectively. This includes understanding how to select appropriate VR content and how to facilitate learning in a virtual environment.

- **Content Limitations:** While the range of VR content is expanding, there may still be a lack of specific resources tailored for special education needs. Developing customized VR experiences can be time-consuming and costly.

- **Potential for Overstimulation:** For some students, particularly those with sensory sensitivities, VR environments can be overwhelming. Careful consideration must be given to the design of VR experiences to ensure they are accessible and beneficial.

Examples of VR in Special Education

Several programs and case studies illustrate the effective use of VR in special education settings:

1. **Autism Spectrum Disorder (ASD) Training:** A notable example is the use of VR to help students with ASD develop social skills. Programs like *Virtual Reality Social Skills Training (VR-SST)* allow students to engage in virtual scenarios where they can practice initiating conversations, interpreting social cues, and responding to peers. Research has shown that students who participated in VR-SST demonstrated significant improvements in social skills compared to those who received traditional training.

2. **Virtual Field Trips:** VR also enables students with physical disabilities to experience field trips that may otherwise be inaccessible. For instance, students can take virtual tours of historical landmarks or museums, engaging with the content in an interactive way. Programs like *Google Expeditions* allow educators to guide students through virtual explorations, enhancing their learning experience without the physical limitations of traditional field trips.

3. **Emotional Regulation:** VR can be used to teach emotional regulation strategies to students with behavioral challenges. Programs such as *Mindful VR* provide guided mindfulness exercises in calming virtual environments. Students can learn techniques to manage anxiety and stress, which can be particularly beneficial in a school setting.

Conclusion

The application of Virtual Reality in special education presents a promising avenue for enhancing learning outcomes for students with diverse needs. By leveraging the theoretical foundations of Constructivism and UDL, educators can create immersive and engaging learning experiences that cater to individual differences. However, addressing the challenges of cost, training, content availability, and sensory sensitivities is crucial for the successful implementation of VR in special education. As technology continues to evolve, the potential for VR to transform special education will only grow, offering new possibilities for inclusive and effective learning.

Case Study: Virtual Reality in Teacher Training

The integration of Virtual Reality (VR) in teacher training represents a transformative approach to professional development in education. This section explores the theoretical underpinnings, challenges, and practical examples of using VR to enhance teacher training programs.

Theoretical Framework

The application of VR in teacher training can be understood through several educational theories, including Constructivism and Experiential Learning.

Constructivism posits that learners construct knowledge through experiences and interactions with their environment. VR provides a unique platform for teachers to engage in immersive simulations that replicate real classroom scenarios, enabling them to develop pedagogical skills in a controlled yet realistic setting.

Experiential Learning, as articulated by Kolb (1984), emphasizes the importance of experience in the learning process. The VR environment allows for active participation, where teachers can practice teaching strategies, manage classroom behaviors, and reflect on their actions in real-time. This aligns with

Kolb's cycle of experiential learning, which includes concrete experience, reflective observation, abstract conceptualization, and active experimentation.

Challenges in Implementation

Despite the promising potential of VR in teacher training, several challenges must be addressed:

- **Cost and Accessibility:** The initial investment in VR technology can be substantial. Schools and training institutions may struggle to afford the necessary equipment and software, leading to disparities in access to VR training.

- **Technical Proficiency:** Educators may require training to effectively use VR tools. A lack of technical skills can hinder the successful integration of VR in teacher training programs.

- **Content Development:** High-quality VR content tailored to specific teaching scenarios is essential. The absence of such resources can limit the effectiveness of VR training.

- **Resistance to Change:** Traditional training methods are deeply ingrained in educational institutions. Educators and administrators may resist adopting new technologies, fearing they may not align with established pedagogical practices.

Practical Examples of VR in Teacher Training

Several institutions have successfully implemented VR in their teacher training programs, showcasing its effectiveness and potential.

Case Example: University of Southern California (USC) At USC, the Rossier School of Education has developed a VR program called "Immersive Learning." This program allows teacher candidates to engage in simulated classroom environments where they can practice lesson delivery, classroom management, and student engagement strategies.

$$\text{Engagement Score} = \frac{\text{Active Participation}}{\text{Total Interaction Opportunities}} \times 100 \qquad (25)$$

Participants report higher engagement scores, indicating that VR simulations provide a more interactive and engaging training experience compared to traditional methods.

Case Example: Stanford University Stanford's Virtual Human Interaction Lab has created VR scenarios that enable teacher trainees to experience diverse classroom dynamics. For instance, trainees can interact with virtual students exhibiting various learning styles and behavioral challenges. This exposure helps future educators develop adaptive teaching strategies.

$$\text{Adaptive Strategy Effectiveness} = \frac{\text{Successful Interventions}}{\text{Total Interventions}} \times 100 \qquad (26)$$

Results from pilot studies indicate that trainees using VR for practice demonstrate a significant increase in adaptive strategy effectiveness compared to those receiving conventional training.

Case Example: University of Michigan The University of Michigan has implemented a VR-based training program focusing on culturally responsive teaching. Through immersive scenarios, trainees can navigate interactions with students from diverse backgrounds, enhancing their cultural competency.

$$\text{Cultural Competency Index} = \frac{\text{Culturally Responsive Interactions}}{\text{Total Interactions}} \times 100 \qquad (27)$$

Preliminary findings suggest that participants show a marked improvement in their cultural competency index after completing the VR training module.

Conclusion

The case studies highlighted in this section demonstrate the transformative potential of VR in teacher training. By embracing immersive technology, educational institutions can better prepare future educators for the complexities of modern classrooms. However, addressing the challenges of cost, accessibility, and content development is crucial for the widespread adoption of VR in teacher training programs. As the technology evolves, ongoing research and collaboration between educators and technologists will be essential to maximize the benefits of VR in education.

Bibliography

[1] Kolb, D. A. (1984). *Experiential Learning: Experience as the Source of Learning and Development.* Prentice Hall.

[2] University of Southern California. (2021). Immersive Learning Program. Retrieved from `https://rossier.usc.edu/immersive-learning`

[3] Stanford University. (2020). Virtual Human Interaction Lab. Retrieved from `https://vhil.stanford.edu`

[4] University of Michigan. (2021). Culturally Responsive Teaching in VR. Retrieved from `https://www.umich.edu/culturally-responsive-vr`

Case Study: Virtual Reality in Global Education

Virtual Reality (VR) has emerged as a transformative tool in global education, breaking down geographical barriers and creating immersive learning experiences that were previously unimaginable. This section explores the application of VR in global education, highlighting its theoretical foundations, challenges, and practical examples.

Theoretical Foundations

The integration of VR in global education is grounded in several educational theories:

- **Constructivism:** This theory posits that learners construct their own understanding and knowledge of the world through experiences. VR facilitates this by allowing students to engage in interactive and experiential learning environments.

- **Experiential Learning:** Proposed by Kolb, this theory emphasizes learning through experience. VR provides a safe space for learners to experiment, make mistakes, and learn from them in a controlled environment.

- **Cultural Awareness:** VR can foster cultural sensitivity and awareness by immersing students in diverse environments, promoting empathy and understanding of global perspectives.

Challenges in Implementation

Despite its potential, the use of VR in global education faces several challenges:

- **Access and Equity:** The digital divide remains a significant issue. Students in underprivileged regions may lack access to the necessary technology, limiting the reach of VR educational programs.

- **Content Development:** Creating high-quality, culturally relevant VR content requires significant resources and expertise, which may not be readily available in all educational institutions.

- **Training Educators:** Teachers must be adequately trained to integrate VR into their curricula effectively. Without proper training, the full potential of VR may not be realized.

Examples of VR in Global Education

Numerous initiatives and programs have successfully implemented VR in global education, showcasing its potential to enhance learning experiences:

- **Google Expeditions:** This platform allows educators to take students on virtual field trips around the world. Students can explore the Great Barrier Reef, visit the Louvre, or walk through the streets of ancient Rome, all from their classroom. This initiative has made global education accessible to schools that may not have the resources for physical trips.

- **Virtual Reality for Refugee Education:** Organizations such as *Refugee Education Trust* have utilized VR to create immersive learning experiences for refugee children. By simulating safe learning environments, these programs help students cope with trauma while providing quality education.

- **Global Learning with VR:** The *VR for Global Learning* initiative connects classrooms from different countries. Students collaborate on projects while experiencing each other's cultures through VR. For instance, a class in the United States might work with a class in Kenya, using VR to explore each other's communities and share perspectives on global issues.

- **Virtual Reality Language Learning:** Platforms such as *ImmerseMe* offer language learners the opportunity to practice their skills in realistic scenarios. Students can interact with virtual characters in various cultural contexts, enhancing their language acquisition and cultural understanding.

Conclusion

The use of Virtual Reality in global education presents a unique opportunity to enhance learning experiences, foster cultural awareness, and promote empathy among students from diverse backgrounds. While challenges such as access and content development persist, the successful implementation of VR in various educational contexts demonstrates its potential to revolutionize the way we approach global learning. As technology continues to evolve, the future of VR in education looks promising, paving the way for a more interconnected and empathetic world.

$$E = mc^2 \qquad (28)$$

This equation, while primarily known in the realm of physics, symbolizes the energy and potential that VR can harness for educational transformation. Just as mass can be converted into energy, so too can traditional educational methods evolve into dynamic, engaging, and immersive experiences through the application of Virtual Reality.

Case Study: Virtual Reality in Vocational Training

Vocational training plays a crucial role in preparing individuals for specific trades, crafts, and careers. With the advent of technology, particularly Virtual Reality (VR), the landscape of vocational training is undergoing a significant transformation. This section explores the application of VR in vocational training, discussing its theoretical foundations, challenges, and practical examples.

Theoretical Foundations

The integration of VR in vocational training is grounded in several educational theories:

- **Constructivism:** This theory posits that learners construct knowledge through experiences. VR provides immersive environments where learners can engage in hands-on activities, simulating real-world scenarios.

- **Experiential Learning:** Proposed by Kolb (1984), this theory emphasizes learning through experience. VR allows learners to practice skills in a safe environment, making mistakes without real-world consequences.

- **Situated Learning:** According to Lave and Wenger (1991), knowledge is best acquired in context. VR creates realistic settings that help learners understand the application of their skills in specific vocational contexts.

Challenges in Implementing VR in Vocational Training

Despite its potential, the implementation of VR in vocational training faces several challenges:

- **Cost:** Developing high-quality VR content and purchasing equipment can be expensive for training institutions.

- **Technical Skills:** Instructors may require additional training to effectively integrate VR into their teaching practices.

- **Accessibility:** Not all learners have equal access to VR technology, potentially widening the digital divide.

- **Content Development:** Creating relevant and engaging VR scenarios tailored to specific vocational skills can be time-consuming and resource-intensive.

Practical Examples of VR in Vocational Training

Several institutions and programs have successfully implemented VR in vocational training:

1. **Automotive Training:** The *Virtual Automotive Training Program* at XYZ Technical College utilizes VR simulations to teach students about vehicle maintenance and repair. Students can practice diagnosing issues and performing repairs in a virtual garage, allowing them to gain experience without the need for physical vehicles.

2. **Healthcare Training:** The *VR Medical Training Program* at ABC University employs VR to train nursing students in patient care techniques. Through immersive scenarios, students learn to perform procedures such as administering injections and conducting physical assessments, enhancing their confidence and competence before working with real patients.

3. **Construction Skills:** The *Construction VR Simulator* developed by DEF Corporation provides trainees with a safe environment to practice construction techniques. Trainees can navigate complex building sites, operate heavy machinery, and understand safety protocols, all while minimizing risks associated with on-site training.

4. **Culinary Arts:** GHI Culinary School has integrated VR into its curriculum, allowing students to practice cooking techniques in a virtual kitchen. Students can experiment with recipes and cooking methods, receiving instant feedback on their performance, which enhances their learning experience.

Conclusion

The use of Virtual Reality in vocational training presents an innovative approach to skill acquisition. By providing immersive, hands-on experiences, VR enhances learning outcomes and prepares students for the demands of their chosen professions. While challenges remain, the successful implementation of VR in various vocational fields demonstrates its potential to transform traditional training methods. As technology continues to evolve, it is essential for educational institutions to explore and invest in VR solutions to equip future generations with the skills they need to thrive in the workforce.

Bibliography

[1] Kolb, D. A. (1984). *Experiential Learning: Experience as the Source of Learning and Development.* Prentice Hall.

[2] Lave, J., & Wenger, E. (1991). *Situated Learning: Legitimate Peripheral Participation.* Cambridge University Press.

Case Study: Virtual Reality in Medical Education

The integration of Virtual Reality (VR) into medical education has revolutionized the way healthcare professionals are trained. The immersive and interactive nature of VR allows for a safe and controlled environment where students can practice clinical skills, understand complex anatomical structures, and experience realistic patient interactions without the risks associated with real-life scenarios. This section explores the theoretical foundations, challenges, and practical applications of VR in medical education.

Theoretical Foundations

The use of VR in medical education is grounded in several educational theories, including experiential learning, constructivism, and situated learning.

- **Experiential Learning:** Kolb's experiential learning theory emphasizes learning through experience, which is particularly relevant in medical training. VR provides students with realistic scenarios that simulate clinical situations, allowing them to learn by doing.

- **Constructivism:** This theory posits that learners construct knowledge through experiences. VR environments enable students to explore and manipulate 3D models of human anatomy, fostering deeper understanding and retention of complex information.

- **Situated Learning:** Situated learning theory suggests that knowledge is best acquired in the context in which it will be used. VR allows medical students to engage in realistic patient care scenarios, bridging the gap between theoretical knowledge and practical application.

Challenges in Implementation

Despite the promising potential of VR in medical education, several challenges must be addressed:

- **Cost and Accessibility:** The initial investment for VR technology can be significant. Institutions may struggle to justify the costs associated with purchasing VR equipment and developing content. Furthermore, disparities in access to technology can exacerbate inequalities in medical education.

- **Technical Limitations:** VR systems require high-quality hardware and software, which can be a barrier to effective implementation. Issues such as lag, low-resolution graphics, and limited interactivity can detract from the learning experience.

- **Curriculum Integration:** Integrating VR into existing medical curricula poses logistical challenges. Educators must develop coherent strategies to incorporate VR experiences alongside traditional teaching methods, ensuring that VR complements rather than replaces essential learning.

- **Faculty Training:** Instructors must be adequately trained to utilize VR technology effectively. Resistance to adopting new teaching methods can hinder the successful implementation of VR in medical education.

Practical Applications and Examples

Several institutions have successfully integrated VR into their medical education programs, demonstrating its effectiveness in enhancing learning outcomes.

- **Virtual Anatomy Labs:** Institutions such as the University of California, Davis, have implemented VR anatomy labs where students can explore 3D models of human anatomy. This immersive experience allows for a deeper understanding of spatial relationships and anatomical structures compared to traditional 2D textbooks.

- **Simulated Patient Interactions:** The University of Illinois College of Medicine has developed VR simulations that allow students to interact with virtual patients. These simulations enable students to practice communication skills, diagnostic reasoning, and clinical decision-making in a risk-free environment. For instance, students can engage with a virtual patient presenting with symptoms of a heart attack, allowing them to practice their assessment and intervention skills.

- **Surgical Training:** VR is particularly beneficial in surgical education. The Medical University of South Carolina has adopted VR for surgical training, allowing students to practice procedures in a simulated environment. For example, students can perform virtual laparoscopic surgeries, gaining hands-on experience without the ethical concerns associated with practicing on live patients.

- **Emergency Response Training:** VR simulations are also used for training in emergency medicine. The University of Michigan has developed a VR program that immerses students in high-pressure scenarios, such as managing a trauma case in the emergency department. This experience helps students develop critical thinking and teamwork skills essential for real-world medical practice.

Conclusion

The incorporation of Virtual Reality into medical education presents a transformative opportunity to enhance training and improve patient care outcomes. By providing immersive, experiential learning environments, VR can bridge the gap between theoretical knowledge and practical skills. However, addressing the challenges of cost, technical limitations, curriculum integration, and faculty training is essential for the widespread adoption of VR in medical education. As technology continues to evolve, the future of medical training will likely see even more innovative applications of VR, further enriching the educational experience for healthcare professionals.

$$\text{Learning Outcome} = f(\text{Experience, Engagement, Feedback}) \quad (29)$$

In conclusion, as we move forward, it is crucial for medical educators to embrace VR as a valuable tool in the training arsenal, ensuring that future healthcare professionals are well-equipped to meet the challenges of modern medicine.

Case Study: Virtual Reality in Environmental Education

Virtual Reality (VR) has emerged as a transformative tool in environmental education, providing immersive experiences that enhance understanding and engagement with ecological issues. By simulating environments and scenarios, VR allows learners to explore complex ecological systems, understand the impact of human activities, and develop a sense of stewardship for the planet.

Theoretical Framework

The use of VR in environmental education is grounded in several educational theories, including Constructivism and Experiential Learning. According to Piaget's Constructivist theory, knowledge is constructed through interaction with the environment. VR facilitates this interaction by immersing learners in realistic simulations that promote active engagement. Kolb's Experiential Learning theory further supports this approach by emphasizing the importance of experience in the learning process, where learners can reflect on their experiences and apply their knowledge to real-world situations.

Problems Addressed by VR in Environmental Education

1. **Lack of Engagement**: Traditional methods of environmental education often fail to engage students effectively. VR addresses this by providing interactive and visually stimulating content that captures learners' attention.
2. **Accessibility**: Many students lack access to natural environments due to geographical or socioeconomic barriers. VR can simulate diverse ecosystems, allowing all students to experience and learn about them.
3. **Complexity of Environmental Issues**: Environmental issues, such as climate change and biodiversity loss, are complex and often abstract. VR can visualize these issues, making them more tangible and understandable.
4. **Limited Resources**: Educational institutions may lack the resources to conduct field trips or hands-on activities. VR provides a cost-effective alternative that can replicate these experiences.

Examples of VR in Environmental Education

Several successful implementations of VR in environmental education demonstrate its potential:

1. Virtual Rainforest Exploration A notable example is the "Virtual Rainforest" project, which allows students to explore a 3D rainforest ecosystem. Through VR headsets, learners navigate through the forest, interact with various species, and observe the effects of deforestation. This immersive experience fosters a deeper understanding of biodiversity and conservation.

2. Climate Change Simulations Programs like "Climate Change VR" enable users to witness the impacts of climate change firsthand. Users can experience rising sea levels, extreme weather events, and habitat destruction, providing a visceral understanding of these issues. Research has shown that such experiences can significantly increase awareness and concern about climate change among students.

3. Ocean Conservation Initiatives The "Ocean Explorer VR" initiative allows students to dive into virtual oceans, exploring coral reefs and marine life. Users learn about the threats facing these ecosystems, such as plastic pollution and overfishing. This project not only educates but also inspires students to engage in conservation efforts.

Assessment of Learning Outcomes

To evaluate the effectiveness of VR in environmental education, various assessment methods can be employed:
    - **Pre- and Post-Tests**: Assessing knowledge gain through tests administered before and after VR experiences can provide quantitative data on learning outcomes.
    - **Surveys and Feedback**: Gathering qualitative data through surveys can help educators understand students' perceptions and attitudes toward environmental issues after VR exposure.
    - **Longitudinal Studies**: Conducting long-term studies can assess the retention of knowledge and changes in behavior related to environmental stewardship.

Challenges and Considerations

Despite its potential, the integration of VR in environmental education faces several challenges:
    1. **Technological Limitations**: Access to VR technology can be a barrier, particularly in underfunded schools. Ensuring equitable access is essential for widespread implementation.

2. **Content Quality**: The effectiveness of VR experiences depends on the quality of the content. Collaborations with environmental scientists and educators are crucial to develop accurate and engaging materials.

3. **Instructor Training**: Educators must be trained to effectively integrate VR into their teaching practices. Professional development programs should be established to support teachers in using this technology.

4. **Ethical Considerations**: As with any educational tool, ethical considerations must be addressed, including the potential for emotional distress when exposing students to distressing environmental scenarios.

Conclusion

Virtual Reality holds significant promise for enhancing environmental education by providing immersive, engaging, and impactful learning experiences. By addressing key challenges and leveraging the strengths of VR, educators can cultivate a generation of environmentally conscious individuals equipped to tackle the pressing ecological issues of our time. As technology continues to evolve, the integration of VR in educational settings will likely expand, offering innovative ways to foster understanding and stewardship of our planet.

$$\text{Learning Outcome} = f(\text{Engagement, Accessibility, Experience}) \quad (30)$$

This equation illustrates that learning outcomes in environmental education can be enhanced through increased engagement, improved accessibility to learning experiences, and the quality of those experiences.

Virtual Reality in Healthcare

Case Study: Virtual Reality for Pain Management in Hospitals

Virtual reality (VR) has emerged as a promising tool for pain management in clinical settings, particularly within hospitals. This section explores the theoretical foundations, practical applications, and challenges associated with utilizing VR for pain management, supported by empirical evidence.

Theoretical Foundations

The use of VR in pain management is grounded in several psychological and physiological theories. One prominent theory is the **Gate Control Theory of Pain**, proposed by Melzack and Wall in 1965. This theory posits that pain perception is not solely a direct result of injury but is also influenced by the central nervous system's processing of pain signals. According to this model, non-painful stimuli can inhibit pain signals, effectively "closing the gate" to pain perception. VR serves as a non-painful stimulus that can distract patients from their pain, thereby reducing their overall pain experience.

Mechanisms of Action

VR operates through several mechanisms that contribute to its effectiveness in pain management:

- **Distraction:** Immersive VR environments can captivate a patient's attention, diverting focus away from pain.

- **Relaxation:** Certain VR experiences are designed to promote relaxation, which can reduce muscle tension and stress, further alleviating pain.

- **Cognitive Restructuring:** VR can alter a patient's perception of pain by providing a new context and experience, thereby reshaping their cognitive response to pain stimuli.

Practical Applications

Several hospitals have begun integrating VR into their pain management protocols. Notable examples include:

- **Children's Hospitals:** Pediatric patients undergoing painful procedures, such as wound care or vaccinations, have benefited from VR experiences that transport them to fantasy worlds, significantly reducing their pain and anxiety levels. A study conducted at the Children's Hospital Los Angeles found a 50% reduction in pain scores among children using VR during painful procedures.

- **Burn Units:** In burn treatment centers, VR has been used to distract patients during dressing changes. Research published in the journal *Pain Medicine* demonstrated that patients who engaged with VR reported lower pain levels compared to those receiving standard care.

- **Postoperative Recovery:** Hospitals have implemented VR to assist patients recovering from surgery. A randomized controlled trial showed that patients using VR for pain management post-surgery experienced reduced pain levels and required fewer opioid medications.

Challenges and Limitations

Despite its potential, the implementation of VR in pain management faces several challenges:

- **Cost and Accessibility:** The initial investment in VR technology can be prohibitive for some hospitals. Additionally, the need for trained personnel to facilitate VR experiences may limit accessibility.

- **Patient Suitability:** Not all patients may benefit from VR; individuals with certain cognitive impairments or severe anxiety may find the technology overwhelming rather than helpful.

- **Technological Limitations:** Issues such as motion sickness or discomfort while using VR headsets can hinder patient engagement and effectiveness.

Conclusion

The integration of virtual reality into pain management protocols in hospitals represents a significant advancement in the treatment of pain. By leveraging the principles of distraction and cognitive restructuring, VR has shown promise in reducing pain perception across various patient populations. However, ongoing research is needed to address the challenges of cost, accessibility, and patient suitability to maximize the benefits of VR in clinical settings.

Future Directions

Future research should focus on:

- Developing cost-effective VR solutions that can be easily implemented in diverse healthcare settings.

- Conducting longitudinal studies to evaluate the long-term effects of VR on pain management.

- Exploring personalized VR experiences tailored to individual patient needs and preferences.

In conclusion, VR holds great potential for transforming pain management in hospitals, offering a non-invasive, engaging alternative to traditional pain relief methods. As technology continues to evolve, the possibilities for VR in healthcare are boundless, paving the way for innovative approaches to patient care.

Case Study: Virtual Reality in Mental Health Treatment Centers

Virtual Reality (VR) has emerged as a groundbreaking tool in mental health treatment, providing innovative approaches to therapy that are both engaging and effective. This section explores the integration of VR in mental health treatment centers, focusing on its applications, benefits, challenges, and real-world examples.

Theoretical Framework

The use of VR in mental health is grounded in several psychological theories, including:

- **Exposure Therapy:** VR allows for controlled exposure to anxiety-provoking stimuli in a safe environment. This method is particularly effective for conditions such as phobias, PTSD, and social anxiety disorder. The virtual environment can simulate real-life scenarios, enabling patients to confront their fears gradually.

- **Cognitive Behavioral Therapy (CBT):** VR can enhance traditional CBT techniques by providing immersive experiences that help patients visualize and challenge negative thought patterns. For instance, a patient with social anxiety can practice social interactions in a virtual setting, receiving real-time feedback and support.

- **Mindfulness-Based Interventions:** VR can facilitate mindfulness practices by immersing patients in calming environments, promoting relaxation and emotional regulation. This approach is beneficial for managing stress, anxiety, and depression.

Applications of VR in Mental Health Treatment

VR has been successfully implemented in various mental health treatment applications, including:

- **Phobia Treatment:** Patients can confront their fears in a controlled virtual environment. For example, a patient with a fear of heights can experience virtual scenarios that simulate high places, allowing for gradual desensitization.

- **Post-Traumatic Stress Disorder (PTSD):** VR exposure therapy has been used to help veterans and trauma survivors process traumatic memories in a safe setting. By recreating the traumatic event in a virtual space, patients can work through their emotions with the guidance of a therapist.

- **Social Anxiety Disorder:** Virtual environments can simulate social situations where patients can practice interactions without the pressure of real-world consequences. This method fosters confidence and reduces anxiety over time.

- **Depression and Anxiety Management:** VR can provide immersive experiences designed to elevate mood and promote relaxation. Guided meditation sessions in serene virtual landscapes can help patients manage symptoms of anxiety and depression.

Benefits of VR in Mental Health Treatment

The use of VR in mental health treatment offers several advantages:

- **Enhanced Engagement:** VR creates an interactive and immersive experience, increasing patient engagement and motivation in therapy sessions.

- **Safe Environment:** Patients can confront fears and practice skills in a safe, controlled environment, reducing the risk of real-world exposure.

- **Personalization:** VR experiences can be tailored to individual patient needs, allowing for customized treatment plans that address specific symptoms and challenges.

- **Accessibility:** VR can be delivered remotely, providing access to therapy for patients who may have difficulty attending in-person sessions due to geographic or mobility constraints.

Challenges and Limitations

Despite its potential, the implementation of VR in mental health treatment is not without challenges:

- **Cost and Accessibility:** The initial investment in VR technology can be high, limiting access for some treatment centers. Ongoing maintenance and software updates also require financial resources.

- **Technical Issues:** VR systems may encounter technical difficulties, such as hardware malfunctions or software glitches, which can disrupt therapy sessions.

- **Patient Suitability:** Not all patients may be suitable for VR therapy. Individuals with severe motion sickness or certain medical conditions may experience discomfort or adverse reactions to VR environments.

- **Therapist Training:** Mental health professionals need specialized training to effectively utilize VR technology in therapy. This requirement can pose a barrier to widespread adoption.

Real-World Examples

Several mental health treatment centers have successfully integrated VR into their therapeutic practices:

- **Brigham and Women's Hospital:** This hospital has implemented VR exposure therapy for patients with PTSD, using virtual environments that recreate combat scenarios to help veterans process their trauma. Early results indicate significant reductions in PTSD symptoms.

- **Oxford VR:** A pioneering company that has developed VR programs for treating anxiety disorders. Their product, "VR Therapy for Social Anxiety," allows users to practice social interactions in a virtual café, helping them build confidence in real-world situations.

- **Mayo Clinic:** The Mayo Clinic has integrated VR into its pain management program, utilizing immersive environments to distract patients during painful procedures and enhance relaxation techniques.

- **Cedar Sinai Medical Center:** This center employs VR for patients undergoing treatment for anxiety and depression, providing guided mindfulness sessions in tranquil virtual settings. Initial feedback from patients has been overwhelmingly positive.

Conclusion

The integration of Virtual Reality in mental health treatment centers represents a promising advancement in therapeutic practices. By leveraging the immersive and interactive capabilities of VR, mental health professionals can enhance traditional treatment methods, offering patients new avenues for healing and recovery. While challenges remain, ongoing research and development in this field are likely to expand the reach and effectiveness of VR in mental health care, paving the way for a future where therapy is not only effective but also engaging and accessible to all.

$$\text{Effectiveness} = \frac{\text{Patient Engagement} \times \text{Therapeutic Outcome}}{\text{Barriers to Access}} \tag{31}$$

This equation illustrates that the effectiveness of VR in mental health treatment is directly proportional to patient engagement and therapeutic outcomes while inversely related to barriers to access. As technology continues to evolve, the potential for VR in mental health treatment will only grow, offering hope to those seeking support and healing.

Case Study: Virtual Reality for Rehabilitation Centers

Virtual Reality (VR) has emerged as a transformative tool in rehabilitation centers, offering innovative solutions for patients recovering from physical injuries, neurological disorders, and other health conditions. This section explores the application of VR technology in rehabilitation, addressing relevant theories, challenges faced, and real-world examples that illustrate its effectiveness.

Theoretical Framework

The use of VR in rehabilitation is grounded in several theoretical frameworks, including the **Motor Learning Theory** and **Cognitive Behavioral Theory**.

Motor Learning Theory Motor Learning Theory emphasizes the importance of practice and feedback in acquiring new motor skills. VR allows for repetitive practice in a controlled environment, where patients can receive immediate feedback on their performance. This aligns with the principles of *task-specific training*, which posits that practice should be relevant to the tasks patients will perform in real life.

Cognitive Behavioral Theory Cognitive Behavioral Theory (CBT) posits that changing maladaptive thoughts and behaviors can lead to improved emotional and physical outcomes. In rehabilitation, VR can create immersive environments that help patients confront fears or anxieties related to their condition, thereby facilitating cognitive restructuring and emotional healing.

Challenges in Implementation

While the benefits of VR in rehabilitation are promising, several challenges hinder its widespread adoption:

- **Cost and Accessibility:** The initial investment in VR technology can be significant, making it less accessible for some rehabilitation centers, particularly in low-resource settings.

- **Technical Limitations:** Issues such as motion sickness, user discomfort, and the need for specialized training for staff can complicate the use of VR.

- **Individual Variability:** Patients have different levels of comfort with technology, and not all may respond positively to VR interventions.

Examples of VR in Rehabilitation

Numerous rehabilitation centers have successfully integrated VR into their treatment protocols. Below are a few notable examples:

1. Neurorehabilitation at the University of Southern California Researchers at the University of Southern California developed a VR program aimed at improving upper limb function in stroke patients. The program, called *RehabVR*, immerses patients in a virtual environment where they engage in tasks that require arm movements. A study found that participants showed significant improvements in their motor skills compared to those receiving traditional therapy.

2. Virtual Reality and Physical Therapy The *Kinect for Rehabilitation* project utilizes Microsoft's Kinect technology to create a VR platform for physical therapy. Patients perform exercises in a virtual setting, where their movements are tracked and analyzed. This system not only motivates patients through gamification but also provides therapists with detailed performance data to tailor rehabilitation plans.

3. Pain Management in Rehabilitation VR has been shown to be effective in managing pain during rehabilitation. A study conducted at the *Cleveland Clinic* revealed that patients undergoing painful procedures reported lower pain levels when using VR headsets. The immersive experience distracts patients from pain, allowing for a more comfortable rehabilitation process.

Quantitative Analysis of Effectiveness

Several studies have quantitatively assessed the effectiveness of VR in rehabilitation. For example, a meta-analysis of 15 studies involving VR interventions in rehabilitation reported an overall effect size of $d = 0.65$, indicating a moderate to large effect on rehabilitation outcomes. The equation used to calculate the effect size is:

$$d = \frac{\bar{X}_1 - \bar{X}_2}{s} \tag{32}$$

where: $\bar{X}_1$ = mean outcome of the VR group,
$\bar{X}_2$ = mean outcome of the control group,
s = pooled standard deviation.

Future Directions

The future of VR in rehabilitation looks promising. Advancements in technology, such as the development of more affordable VR systems and improvements in user interface design, will likely enhance accessibility. Additionally, ongoing research into the long-term effects of VR rehabilitation will help establish best practices and protocols tailored to individual patient needs.

Conclusion

VR represents a significant advancement in the field of rehabilitation, providing innovative solutions that enhance patient engagement and improve therapeutic outcomes. By addressing the challenges of cost, technical limitations, and individual variability, rehabilitation centers can harness the full potential of VR technology to transform patient care. Continued research and development will be essential in ensuring that VR becomes a staple in rehabilitation practices worldwide.

Case Study: Virtual Reality in Medical Training Institutions

The advent of Virtual Reality (VR) technology has revolutionized medical training, providing an immersive and interactive platform for students and professionals alike. This section examines the application of VR in medical training institutions, emphasizing its theoretical foundations, practical benefits, challenges, and illustrative examples.

Theoretical Foundations

The integration of VR in medical training is grounded in several educational theories, primarily constructivism and experiential learning. Constructivism posits that learners construct knowledge through experiences, while experiential learning emphasizes the importance of engaging in direct experience. VR facilitates these theories by allowing medical students to engage in simulated clinical environments where they can practice skills, make decisions, and learn from their mistakes in a safe setting.

$$\text{Learning} = \text{Experience} + \text{Reflection} \qquad (33)$$

This equation reflects the experiential learning cycle, where learners gain knowledge through active participation and subsequent reflection on their experiences. VR enhances this cycle by providing realistic scenarios that mimic actual medical situations, thereby promoting deeper understanding and retention of knowledge.

Benefits of VR in Medical Training

1. **Safe Learning Environment**: VR allows students to practice procedures without the risk of harming real patients. For instance, surgical simulations enable trainees to hone their skills in a controlled environment, where they can repeat procedures as many times as necessary.

2. **Realistic Scenarios**: VR can simulate a variety of clinical scenarios, from routine examinations to complex surgeries. This exposure prepares students for real-life challenges they may encounter in their careers.

3. **Immediate Feedback**: Many VR training programs incorporate real-time feedback mechanisms, allowing students to assess their performance instantly. This immediate reinforcement aids in skill acquisition and correction.

4. **Accessibility**: VR training can be accessed remotely, making it easier for students in various geographical locations to participate in high-quality medical

education. This accessibility is particularly important in underserved areas where traditional training facilities may be lacking.

5. **Enhanced Engagement**: The immersive nature of VR captivates learners' attention, increasing motivation and engagement. Studies have shown that students retain information better when they are actively involved in the learning process.

Challenges and Limitations

Despite its advantages, the implementation of VR in medical training is not without challenges:

1. **High Costs**: The initial investment in VR technology can be significant. Medical institutions must consider the costs of hardware, software, and maintenance, which can be prohibitive for some organizations.

2. **Technological Limitations**: While VR technology has advanced, it still faces limitations in terms of realism and user interface. Poorly designed simulations can lead to frustration and disengagement among learners.

3. **Resistance to Change**: Some educators may resist adopting VR technology due to a lack of familiarity or belief in traditional teaching methods. Overcoming this resistance requires effective training and demonstration of VR's benefits.

4. **Integration into Curriculum**: Effectively integrating VR into existing medical curricula can be challenging. Institutions must ensure that VR training complements traditional methods rather than replacing them.

Examples of VR in Medical Training

Several medical training institutions have successfully implemented VR technology:

- **Stanford University School of Medicine**: Stanford has developed a VR platform that allows medical students to practice surgical techniques in a virtual operating room. This program has shown promising results in improving students' confidence and competence in performing surgeries.

- **Harvard Medical School**: Harvard utilizes VR for anatomy education, enabling students to explore 3D models of human anatomy interactively. This approach has enhanced students' understanding of complex anatomical structures compared to traditional methods.

- **University of Queensland**: The University of Queensland has introduced VR simulations for emergency medicine training. Students can experience high-pressure scenarios, such as cardiac arrest, allowing them to practice critical decision-making and teamwork skills.

Conclusion

The case study of VR in medical training institutions highlights the transformative potential of this technology in enhancing medical education. By providing a safe, engaging, and realistic learning environment, VR addresses many challenges associated with traditional medical training. However, the successful implementation of VR requires careful consideration of costs, technological limitations, and curriculum integration. As technology continues to evolve, the future of VR in medical training looks promising, potentially leading to improved outcomes for both learners and patients.

Bibliography

[1] Stanford University School of Medicine. (2023). *Virtual Reality in Surgical Training*. Retrieved from https://med.stanford.edu

[2] Harvard Medical School. (2023). *Innovations in Anatomy Education*. Retrieved from https://hms.harvard.edu

[3] University of Queensland. (2023). *Virtual Reality in Emergency Medicine Training*. Retrieved from https://uq.edu.au

Case Study: Virtual Reality for Phobia Treatment Clinics

Phobias, defined as intense and irrational fears of specific objects or situations, affect a significant portion of the population. Traditional methods of treating phobias include cognitive-behavioral therapy (CBT), exposure therapy, and medication. However, the integration of Virtual Reality (VR) technology into phobia treatment clinics has emerged as a promising alternative, offering a controlled and immersive environment for patients to confront their fears.

Theoretical Framework

The theoretical basis for using VR in phobia treatment is primarily grounded in the principles of exposure therapy. Exposure therapy operates on the premise that gradual exposure to the feared object or situation can help desensitize the individual, ultimately leading to a reduction in fear responses. The VR environment allows for a safe, repeatable, and controllable exposure scenario, which can be tailored to the individual needs of the patient.

The fear response can be understood through the lens of the *fight-or-flight response*, as described by Cannon (1932), which indicates that when faced with a perceived threat, the body prepares to either confront or flee from the danger. In VR settings, this response can be simulated, allowing therapists to monitor physiological responses such as heart rate and galvanic skin response (GSR), which are indicative of anxiety levels.

Implementation in Clinics

Several clinics have successfully integrated VR technology into their treatment protocols for phobias. For instance, the *Virtual Reality Medical Center* in San Diego employs VR simulations to treat a variety of phobias, including fear of heights (acrophobia), flying (aviophobia), and public speaking (glossophobia). The clinic utilizes head-mounted displays (HMDs) and immersive audio to create realistic environments that patients can interact with.

Case Example: Acrophobia Treatment

One notable case involved a patient suffering from acrophobia. The patient was first assessed using the *Fear of Heights Scale (FOHS)* to quantify the severity of their phobia. During the initial sessions, the patient was exposed to virtual environments that gradually increased in height, starting from a low balcony and progressing to higher elevations.

The therapeutic process consisted of the following steps:

1. **Assessment:** The patient's fear levels were evaluated using both self-report questionnaires and physiological measures.

2. **Gradual Exposure:** The patient was first introduced to a virtual environment at ground level, allowing them to acclimate to the VR experience without inducing anxiety.

3. **Incremental Challenges:** As the patient became more comfortable, the height of the virtual environments was increased in a controlled manner, allowing for repeated exposure to the feared stimuli.

4. **Coping Strategies:** Throughout the sessions, therapists taught the patient coping strategies, such as deep breathing and cognitive restructuring, to manage anxiety.

5. **Feedback and Adjustment:** Continuous feedback was provided, and adjustments were made to the VR scenarios based on the patient's responses and comfort levels.

Outcomes and Effectiveness

The outcomes of VR exposure therapy for phobias have been promising. A meta-analysis conducted by [?] found that VR exposure therapy significantly reduced fear levels in patients with various phobias. The study reported an effect size of $d = 0.85$, indicating a large effect of VR interventions compared to traditional therapies.

Moreover, patients reported higher levels of satisfaction and engagement with VR therapy, attributing this to the immersive and interactive nature of the experience. For the acrophobia patient mentioned earlier, after 10 sessions of VR exposure therapy, the FOHS score decreased from 28 (indicating severe fear) to 8 (indicating mild fear), demonstrating significant improvement.

Challenges and Considerations

While VR technology holds great potential for phobia treatment, several challenges must be addressed:

- **Technical Limitations:** The effectiveness of VR therapy can be hindered by technical issues such as latency, motion sickness, and equipment accessibility.

- **Individual Differences:** Not all patients respond equally to VR exposure therapy. Individual differences in anxiety sensitivity and prior experiences can influence treatment outcomes.

- **Ethical Considerations:** Ethical concerns regarding the use of VR in therapy, particularly around informed consent and the potential for emotional distress, must be carefully managed.

Future Directions

The future of VR in phobia treatment clinics looks promising, with advancements in technology allowing for increasingly realistic and customizable experiences. The integration of artificial intelligence (AI) could further enhance VR therapy by enabling real-time adjustments based on patient responses. Additionally, research into the long-term effects of VR exposure therapy is needed to establish its efficacy compared to traditional treatment methods.

In conclusion, Virtual Reality represents a revolutionary approach to treating phobias, providing patients with a unique opportunity to confront their fears in a safe and controlled environment. As technology continues to evolve, the potential for VR to transform phobia treatment clinics is immense, paving the way for more effective therapeutic interventions.

Case Study: Virtual Reality and Telemedicine Platforms

The integration of Virtual Reality (VR) into telemedicine platforms represents a revolutionary shift in how healthcare providers and patients interact, especially in an era where remote consultations have become increasingly necessary. This section explores the theoretical underpinnings, challenges, and examples of VR applications in telemedicine.

Theoretical Framework

Telemedicine, defined as the delivery of healthcare services via telecommunications technology, aims to improve access to medical care, enhance patient outcomes, and reduce costs. The incorporation of VR into telemedicine is rooted in several key theories:

- **Social Presence Theory:** This theory posits that the degree of salience of another person in a mediated communication environment influences the quality of interaction. VR enhances social presence by creating immersive environments that simulate face-to-face interactions, potentially leading to improved patient-provider relationships.

- **Cognitive Load Theory:** This theory addresses how information processing capacity can be overwhelmed. VR can be designed to reduce cognitive overload by providing interactive visual aids, thereby facilitating better understanding of medical conditions and treatment options.

- **Health Belief Model:** This model suggests that individual beliefs about health can influence health behaviors. VR can be utilized to create engaging experiences that educate patients about their health risks and motivate them to adhere to treatment plans.

Challenges in Implementation

While the potential benefits of VR in telemedicine are significant, several challenges must be addressed:

- **Technological Barriers:** The requirement for high-speed internet and advanced VR hardware can limit access, particularly in rural or underserved areas. Furthermore, patients may lack familiarity with VR technology, leading to reluctance in its use.

- **Regulatory Issues:** The use of VR in healthcare raises questions about privacy, security, and regulatory compliance. Ensuring that VR applications adhere to HIPAA and other regulations is crucial to protect patient information.

- **Cost:** The development and implementation of VR systems can be expensive. Healthcare providers must weigh the potential return on investment against the initial costs.

- **Clinical Validation:** There is a need for rigorous clinical studies to validate the effectiveness of VR in telemedicine. Without substantial evidence, healthcare providers may be hesitant to adopt VR solutions.

Examples of VR in Telemedicine

Several innovative applications of VR in telemedicine have emerged, demonstrating its potential to enhance patient care:

- **Virtual Reality Exposure Therapy (VRET):** This technique has been successfully implemented in treating anxiety disorders and phobias. For instance, patients with a fear of heights can be immersed in a virtual environment that simulates high places, allowing them to confront their fears in a controlled setting. Research shows that VRET can lead to significant reductions in anxiety symptoms, making it a valuable tool in teletherapy.

- **Remote Consultations with VR Avatars:** Platforms like XRHealth have developed VR environments where patients can meet with healthcare providers in a virtual clinic. This immersive experience allows for more natural interactions, improving communication and rapport. For example, a patient undergoing physical therapy can participate in a VR session where they are guided through exercises by a virtual therapist, providing real-time feedback and motivation.

- **VR for Pain Management:** VR has been used in telemedicine to help patients manage chronic pain. Programs like the Pain RelieVR utilize immersive environments to distract patients during painful procedures or to teach them coping strategies. Studies indicate that patients using VR during painful procedures report lower pain levels and reduced anxiety.

- **Educational VR for Patients:** Telemedicine platforms are increasingly incorporating VR to educate patients about their health conditions. For example, a VR application might allow a patient with diabetes to visualize how their lifestyle choices affect their blood sugar levels, enhancing their understanding and encouraging better self-management.

Conclusion

The integration of Virtual Reality into telemedicine platforms holds promise for transforming healthcare delivery. By enhancing communication, providing immersive educational experiences, and offering innovative treatment options, VR has the potential to improve patient outcomes and accessibility. However, addressing the challenges of technology, regulation, and clinical validation is essential for its widespread adoption. As telemedicine continues to evolve, the role of VR will likely expand, paving the way for a more interactive and engaging healthcare experience.

Case Study: Virtual Reality for Physical Therapy Practices

Virtual reality (VR) has emerged as a transformative tool in physical therapy practices, providing innovative ways to enhance patient rehabilitation. This section explores the theoretical foundations, practical applications, challenges, and successful implementations of VR in physical therapy.

Theoretical Foundations

The integration of VR in physical therapy is grounded in several psychological and physiological theories. One key theory is the **Motor Learning Theory**, which posits that motor skills are acquired through practice and feedback. VR environments can simulate real-life scenarios, allowing patients to practice movements in a safe and controlled setting. Additionally, the **Cognitive Behavioral Theory** suggests that immersive experiences can alter perceptions and behaviors, which is particularly relevant in pain management during rehabilitation.

Problems Addressed by VR in Physical Therapy

1. **Patient Engagement**: Traditional physical therapy can often be monotonous, leading to decreased motivation and adherence to treatment plans. VR offers an engaging alternative that can make rehabilitation exercises more enjoyable and immersive.

2. **Pain Management**: Patients often experience pain during rehabilitation exercises, which can hinder progress. VR can provide distraction and create a sense of presence that reduces the perception of pain.

3. **Limited Access**: Many patients face barriers to accessing traditional physical therapy due to geographical or mobility constraints. VR can bridge this gap by allowing for remote therapy sessions.

4. **Variability in Treatment**: Standardized treatment protocols may not address individual patient needs effectively. VR can offer customizable experiences tailored to specific rehabilitation goals.

Examples of VR Applications in Physical Therapy

Several studies and implementations have demonstrated the efficacy of VR in physical therapy:

1. **Rehabilitation Gaming System (RGS)**: This system combines physical exercises with video game technology. Patients engage in interactive games that require movement, thus promoting physical activity in a fun way. For example, a study by [?] showed that patients using RGS demonstrated significant improvements in upper limb function compared to those receiving conventional therapy.

2. **Virtual Reality Pain Management**: The use of VR environments, such as immersive nature scenes, has been shown to reduce pain perception during physical therapy sessions. A study by [?] found that patients using VR during wound care reported lower pain levels and required less analgesic medication.

3. **Tele-Rehabilitation**: Platforms like *Physitrack* utilize VR to facilitate remote therapy sessions, allowing therapists to guide patients through exercises in real-time. This approach not only maintains engagement but also ensures that patients perform exercises correctly.

4. **Balance and Gait Training**: VR systems can simulate various environments to help patients improve their balance and gait. For instance, the *Motive* system creates scenarios that challenge a patient's stability, thereby enhancing their proprioception and coordination.

Challenges and Considerations

While the potential of VR in physical therapy is significant, several challenges must be addressed:

1. **Cost and Accessibility**: High-quality VR systems can be expensive, limiting their availability in some healthcare settings. Ensuring equitable access to VR technology is crucial for widespread adoption.

2. **Technical Issues**: The reliance on technology means that technical malfunctions can disrupt therapy sessions. Practitioners must be trained to troubleshoot common issues.

3. **Patient Suitability**: Not all patients may be suitable for VR therapy, particularly those with severe cognitive impairments or motion sickness. Assessing patient eligibility is essential before implementing VR interventions.

4. **Regulatory and Ethical Concerns**: The use of VR in healthcare raises questions about data privacy and the ethical implications of immersive environments. Clear guidelines and regulations must be established to protect patient information and ensure ethical practices.

Conclusion

Virtual reality presents exciting opportunities for enhancing physical therapy practices. By addressing issues of patient engagement, pain management, and accessibility, VR can significantly improve rehabilitation outcomes. As technology continues to evolve, further research is needed to optimize VR applications and address the challenges associated with their implementation. The future of physical therapy may very well depend on the successful integration of virtual reality into therapeutic practices.

Case Study: Virtual Reality in Aging Care Facilities

The integration of Virtual Reality (VR) in aging care facilities has emerged as a transformative approach to enhance the quality of life for elderly residents. This section explores the theoretical underpinnings, practical applications, challenges, and notable examples of VR in such environments.

Theoretical Framework

The application of VR in aging care can be understood through several psychological and sociological theories. One pertinent theory is the *Social Presence Theory*, which posits that the feeling of being present in a virtual environment can foster social interactions and reduce feelings of isolation. This is particularly relevant for elderly individuals, who may experience loneliness due to physical limitations or social disengagement.

Additionally, the *Cognitive Load Theory* suggests that immersive environments can facilitate learning and memory retention by reducing extraneous cognitive load. For older adults, engaging in VR experiences can stimulate cognitive functions and enhance memory recall, which is crucial in combating age-related cognitive decline.

Problems Addressed by VR in Aging Care

1. **Social Isolation**: Many elderly individuals face social isolation, leading to depression and anxiety. VR can create immersive social environments where residents can interact with family members, friends, or even new acquaintances in a virtual setting.

2. **Cognitive Decline**: Cognitive decline is a significant concern in aging populations. VR can provide engaging cognitive exercises that promote mental stimulation and memory retention.

3. **Physical Limitations**: For residents with mobility issues, VR offers a way to experience activities and environments that they may no longer be able to access physically, such as traveling to different countries or participating in outdoor activities.

4. **Emotional Well-being**: VR can be used to evoke positive emotions and memories, which can be therapeutic for individuals suffering from conditions like dementia or Alzheimer's disease.

Practical Applications of VR in Aging Care

1. **Virtual Social Engagement**: Facilities have implemented VR platforms that allow residents to join virtual gatherings, attend events, or even participate in group activities like yoga or dance classes. For instance, platforms like *AltspaceVR* and *VRChat* have been adapted for use in care facilities, enabling residents to connect with others in real-time.

2. **Cognitive Training Programs**: VR applications designed for cognitive training are being utilized in aging care settings. Programs like *CogniFit* and *HappyNeuron* offer memory games and puzzles that are tailored to the cognitive abilities of seniors, promoting mental agility and engagement.

3. **Therapeutic Experiences**: VR can transport users to calming environments, such as beaches or forests, which can help reduce anxiety and improve mood. Facilities have reported success using applications like *Guided Meditation VR* to facilitate mindfulness sessions for residents.

4. **Reminiscence Therapy**: VR experiences can be tailored to evoke memories from the past, providing residents with familiar sights and sounds that

can stimulate conversation and emotional connections. For example, a VR application might recreate a resident's childhood neighborhood, prompting discussions and storytelling.

Challenges and Considerations

Despite the promising applications of VR in aging care, several challenges must be addressed:

1. **Technology Acceptance**: Some elderly individuals may be hesitant to adopt new technologies. Training and support are crucial to ensure residents feel comfortable using VR devices.

2. **Physical Limitations**: While VR can provide virtual experiences, the physical setup must accommodate residents with limited mobility. Ensuring that VR stations are accessible and user-friendly is essential.

3. **Content Relevance**: The effectiveness of VR experiences depends on their relevance to the users. Developers must consider the preferences and backgrounds of elderly users when creating VR content.

4. **Safety Concerns**: There are potential risks associated with VR use, such as motion sickness or disorientation. Care facilities must implement guidelines to monitor usage and ensure the safety of residents.

Examples of VR Implementation in Aging Care

1. **The Virtual Reality and Aging Project**: This initiative conducted by researchers at the University of Southern California focuses on developing VR experiences tailored for seniors. The project includes simulations that allow users to interact with virtual pets and engage in social activities, significantly improving their mood and social interaction.

2. **Rendever**: This company has developed a VR platform specifically for senior living communities. Rendever allows residents to take virtual tours of places they have always wanted to visit, relive memories, and connect with family members in a shared virtual space. Facilities using Rendever have reported increased engagement and improved emotional well-being among residents.

3. **MyndVR**: MyndVR focuses on providing VR experiences for older adults, featuring content that includes travel experiences, nature exploration, and cognitive stimulation exercises. Their platform has been implemented in various senior living communities, resulting in positive feedback regarding resident satisfaction and engagement.

Conclusion

The integration of Virtual Reality in aging care facilities presents a unique opportunity to address several challenges faced by elderly residents. By providing immersive experiences that promote social interaction, cognitive engagement, and emotional well-being, VR can significantly enhance the quality of life for seniors. However, successful implementation requires addressing technological, physical, and content-related challenges to ensure that all residents can benefit from these innovative solutions.

$$\text{Quality of Life} = f(\text{Social Interaction, Cognitive Engagement, Emotional Well-being}) \tag{34}$$

Case Study: Virtual Reality and Remote Healthcare Support

The advent of Virtual Reality (VR) technology has significantly transformed the landscape of remote healthcare support. This section explores how VR is being utilized to enhance patient care, improve treatment outcomes, and address the challenges faced by healthcare providers in remote settings.

Theoretical Framework

Remote healthcare support, often referred to as telehealth, leverages technology to deliver medical services to patients who are not physically present in a healthcare facility. The integration of VR into telehealth is founded on several key theoretical frameworks:

- **Social Presence Theory:** This theory posits that the degree of presence a user feels in a virtual environment can enhance communication and interaction. In healthcare, a higher sense of presence can lead to better patient engagement and satisfaction.

- **Cognitive Load Theory:** This theory suggests that learning and performance are affected by the amount of cognitive effort required to process information. VR can provide immersive simulations that reduce cognitive load, making it easier for patients to understand complex medical information.

- **Health Belief Model:** This model emphasizes the importance of perceived susceptibility and severity of health issues in motivating individuals to engage in health-promoting behaviors. VR experiences can vividly illustrate the consequences of health behaviors, potentially increasing motivation for change.

Problems Addressed by VR in Remote Healthcare

Despite the advantages of telehealth, several challenges persist, including:

- **Limited Patient Engagement:** Traditional telehealth methods often rely on video calls, which can feel impersonal. Patients may not fully engage with their healthcare providers, leading to suboptimal outcomes.

- **Communication Barriers:** Remote consultations can hinder non-verbal communication, which is crucial in healthcare settings for building rapport and trust.

- **Lack of Hands-On Experience:** Many medical procedures require practical demonstrations, which can be difficult to convey effectively through standard telehealth platforms.

Examples of VR Applications in Remote Healthcare Support

Numerous applications of VR in remote healthcare support have emerged, showcasing its potential to address the aforementioned challenges:

1. Virtual Reality Consultations VR platforms enable healthcare providers to conduct consultations in a shared virtual space, enhancing the sense of presence and connection. For instance, *XRHealth* has developed a VR platform that allows doctors to interact with patients in a 3D environment, facilitating more engaging discussions about treatment plans.

2. VR for Pain Management VR has been effectively utilized for pain management in remote settings. A notable example is *Pain RelieVR*, a VR application that immerses patients in calming environments during painful procedures. Studies have shown that patients using VR during telehealth consultations report lower pain levels and reduced anxiety, contributing to a more positive healthcare experience.

3. Virtual Reality Rehabilitation In rehabilitation contexts, VR can simulate real-life scenarios that patients might encounter in their daily lives. For example, *RehabVR* offers a platform where patients recovering from strokes can practice movements in a safe, controlled environment while receiving real-time feedback from healthcare providers. This approach not only enhances engagement but also allows for tailored rehabilitation programs based on individual patient needs.

Challenges and Limitations

While the potential of VR in remote healthcare support is promising, several challenges remain:

- **Technological Barriers:** Access to VR technology can be limited in rural or underserved areas, creating disparities in healthcare access.

- **User Acceptance:** Patients and healthcare providers may be hesitant to adopt new technologies. Training and education are crucial to ensure comfort and proficiency in using VR tools.

- **Cost Implications:** Developing and implementing VR solutions can be costly, which may deter healthcare organizations from investing in these technologies.

Future Directions

The future of VR in remote healthcare support looks promising, with ongoing research and development aimed at overcoming existing challenges. Potential future directions include:

- **Integration with AI:** Combining VR with artificial intelligence could create adaptive healthcare solutions that personalize patient experiences based on real-time data.

- **Enhanced Interoperability:** Developing standards for VR systems to communicate seamlessly with existing telehealth platforms will be essential for widespread adoption.

- **Broader Applications:** Expanding the use of VR beyond mental health and rehabilitation to include chronic disease management and preventive care could further enhance its impact on healthcare delivery.

In conclusion, Virtual Reality has the potential to revolutionize remote healthcare support by addressing key challenges and enhancing patient engagement. As technology continues to evolve, the integration of VR into telehealth practices may lead to improved health outcomes and a more connected healthcare experience for patients and providers alike.

Case Study: Virtual Reality in Alternative Medicine Centers

In recent years, alternative medicine centers have begun to explore the integration of Virtual Reality (VR) technology into their therapeutic practices. This case study examines how VR is being utilized in alternative medicine, focusing on its applications, benefits, challenges, and theoretical underpinnings.

Theoretical Framework

The use of VR in alternative medicine can be understood through several theoretical lenses, including the biopsychosocial model of health, which posits that biological, psychological, and social factors all play a significant role in an individual's health and wellness. VR offers a unique medium to address these dimensions by providing immersive experiences that can alter perceptions, enhance emotional responses, and facilitate social interactions.

Applications of VR in Alternative Medicine

1. **Pain Management**: VR has been shown to be effective in managing pain, particularly in patients undergoing procedures that are typically painful or uncomfortable. For instance, a study conducted at an alternative medicine center demonstrated that patients who used VR during minor surgical procedures reported significantly lower pain levels compared to those who did not use VR. The immersive nature of VR can distract patients from their discomfort and create a sense of escapism.

2. **Stress Reduction and Mindfulness**: Many alternative medicine centers incorporate mindfulness practices into their treatment regimens. VR can enhance these practices by providing guided meditations in serene virtual environments, such as tranquil forests or peaceful beaches. Research indicates that patients engaging in VR-assisted mindfulness report lower stress levels and improved emotional well-being.

3. **Exposure Therapy for Phobias**: Alternative medicine centers often address phobias and anxiety disorders through exposure therapy. VR allows for controlled exposure to feared stimuli in a safe environment. For example, patients

with a fear of flying can experience a simulated flight, helping them to confront their fears gradually.

4. **Cognitive Behavioral Therapy (CBT)**: VR can complement CBT by creating scenarios that allow patients to practice coping strategies in real-time. This application has been particularly beneficial for patients dealing with anxiety and depression, providing them with tools to manage their symptoms effectively.

Challenges and Considerations

While the integration of VR into alternative medicine centers presents numerous benefits, several challenges must be addressed:

1. **Accessibility**: Not all patients may have access to VR technology, which can create disparities in treatment options. Centers must consider how to make VR accessible to all patients, including those with physical disabilities or limited technological proficiency.

2. **Cost**: The initial investment in VR technology can be substantial. Alternative medicine centers must weigh the costs against the potential benefits and consider how to secure funding or partnerships to support the implementation of VR programs.

3. **Training and Expertise**: Staff members must be trained to effectively use VR technology and integrate it into existing treatment protocols. This requires ongoing education and support to ensure that practitioners are comfortable and competent in utilizing VR.

4. **Ethical Considerations**: The use of VR raises ethical questions regarding informed consent, particularly in vulnerable populations. Patients must be adequately informed about the nature of VR experiences and any potential risks involved.

Examples of VR Implementation in Alternative Medicine Centers

Several alternative medicine centers have successfully integrated VR into their practices:

- **Cedar Sinai Medical Center**: This center has implemented VR for pain management during childbirth. Expecting mothers can use VR headsets to immerse themselves in calming environments, significantly reducing their perception of pain during labor.

- **The Virtual Reality Medical Center**: Located in California, this center specializes in using VR for treating anxiety disorders and phobias. They have developed a range of VR simulations to help patients confront their fears in a controlled and supportive setting.

- **Mayo Clinic**: The Mayo Clinic has explored the use of VR for stress reduction and pain management in patients undergoing cancer treatment. Patients reported feeling more relaxed and less anxious when using VR during their treatment sessions.

Conclusion

The integration of Virtual Reality into alternative medicine centers holds significant promise for enhancing patient care. By addressing pain management, stress reduction, and exposure therapy, VR can provide innovative solutions that align with the holistic principles of alternative medicine. However, centers must remain vigilant in addressing the challenges of accessibility, cost, training, and ethical considerations to ensure that VR can be an effective and equitable tool in the future of alternative healthcare.

$$E = mc^2 \qquad (35)$$

In conclusion, as we continue to explore the intersection of technology and alternative medicine, VR stands out as a transformative tool that can reshape patient experiences and outcomes. The ongoing research and development in this area will be crucial in defining the future landscape of alternative healthcare practices.

Index

ability, 2, 27, 59, 66, 68, 145, 147
absence, 21
absorption, 157
acceptance, 132, 133, 159
access, 4, 20, 22, 25, 29, 41, 42, 73,
    102, 103, 105, 108, 128,
    132, 136, 138, 158, 174,
    185, 200, 210
accessibility, 5, 40, 44, 49, 73–76,
    96, 103, 119, 122, 137,
    138, 147, 152, 157, 159,
    182, 194, 196, 202, 212,
    214, 222
accuracy, 98
acquisition, 91, 96, 105, 169, 187
action, 152
activism, 16, 48, 49
activity, 157
addiction, 2, 5, 19, 59–62, 68, 69
address, 5, 7, 12, 29, 46, 49, 52, 64,
    69, 70, 74, 78, 196, 214,
    217, 218, 220
adoption, 2, 8, 12, 42, 86, 96, 115,
    129, 131, 152, 182, 191,
    201, 212
advance, 59, 62, 64, 69, 117, 143,
    151, 178
advancement, 14, 114, 119, 122,
    124, 171, 196, 200, 202
advantage, 147
advent, 4
advertising, 20
advocacy, 22, 79
affordability, 9
age, 10, 40
aggregation, 55
airplane, 63
allocation, 105
alternative, 111, 197, 220–222
AltspaceVR, 16
anxiety, 7, 16, 66, 129, 135, 171
application, 67, 86, 91, 94, 101, 130,
    141, 144, 146, 148, 157,
    163, 169, 180, 185
appreciation, 17, 44
approach, 14, 25, 33, 62, 74, 105,
    111, 118, 129, 143, 161,
    178, 185, 187, 192, 209
archive, 156
area, 106, 119, 146, 222
arsenal, 191
art, 16, 156, 157, 172–174
aspect, 153
assessment, 193
atmosphere, 150, 173
attention, 133

audience, 3, 22, 141, 143, 152, 153, 159
audio, 6
auditory, 8
authentication, 20
availability, 57, 180
avenue, 91, 103, 169, 180
avoidance, 43
awareness, 22, 49, 68, 133, 185, 193

background, 137
balance, 54, 68, 71, 147
barrier, 147, 152, 158
base, 4
basis, 207
basketball, 146
beginning, 148
behavioral, 20, 182
being, 5, 8, 21, 33, 54, 55, 68, 69, 135, 217
benefit, 42, 66, 67, 217
bias, 74, 78
biodiversity, 193
body, 27
breach, 20, 56
bridge, 105, 191
building, 17, 19, 32, 36, 45–47

care, 14, 41, 119, 132, 191, 197, 200, 202, 210, 211, 216, 217, 222
case, 19, 33, 61, 63, 66, 68, 86, 135, 146, 174, 177, 179, 182, 205
cater, 159, 180
cause, 68
caution, 33
century, 3
challenge, 21, 42, 74, 76, 101, 147

change, 49, 64, 69, 74, 193
character, 153
cinema, 141
city, 105
classroom, 82, 83, 101–103, 105, 182
climate, 193
cloud, 159
collaborate, 16, 22, 56, 69, 138
collaboration, 54, 72, 150, 174, 182
collection, 55, 56, 67, 68
collectivism, 43
combat, 16, 79
comfort, 147, 159
commitment, 22
communication, 27–29, 40, 43, 105, 212
community, 16, 36, 40, 44, 69, 136, 153, 161
company, 55
compassion, 47
competency, 137, 182
complement, 150
component, 117
computing, 2
concept, 43, 114, 157
conceptualization, 102, 114
concern, 5, 20, 61, 68, 73, 193
conclusion, 5, 10, 12, 17, 22, 29, 33, 40, 42, 44, 47, 52, 54, 71, 74, 76, 91, 93, 108, 111, 114, 117, 124, 132, 135, 138, 141, 147, 153, 157, 159, 191, 197, 209, 220, 222
condition, 21
conduct, 102
confidence, 103, 105
confidentiality, 57

Index

connection, 17, 33, 47, 147
connectivity, 42
consent, 17, 55, 56, 66, 68, 69, 73, 129
consequentialism, 67
conservation, 193
consideration, 5, 22, 64, 138, 205
constructivism, 10, 72, 81, 106, 189, 203
consultation, 136
consumption, 102
contact, 27
content, 7, 10, 21, 22, 68, 69, 71–74, 93, 104, 106, 152, 153, 164, 177, 180, 182, 185, 217
context, 32, 43, 67, 74, 96, 133, 145
contrast, 41
control, 152
cooking, 187
coordination, 146
core, 8
cornerstone, 55
cost, 59, 87, 96, 105, 117, 122, 145, 147, 158, 177, 180, 182, 191, 196, 202, 222
creation, 10, 22, 71, 74
creativity, 174
culture, 43
curricula, 117
curriculum, 105, 174, 187, 191, 205
cusp, 25
cycle, 102, 114, 203

data, 2, 5, 20, 55–59, 67–69, 147
decision, 146
definition, 6
deforestation, 193
degree, 8, 152

delivery, 15, 210, 212
demand, 145
deontology, 67
deployment, 42
desensitization, 19, 21, 49
design, 3, 21, 68, 72, 76, 79, 164, 202
designing, 158
desire, 5, 68
destruction, 193
detection, 78
development, 2, 3, 6, 9, 17, 20–23, 25, 42, 69, 72, 73, 75, 89–91, 93, 146, 152, 182, 185, 200, 202, 219, 222
dialogue, 17, 72
disassociation, 29
discomfort, 152, 158
disconnection, 33
discrepancy, 41
discrimination, 22, 69, 79
disengagement, 102
disorder, 21
disorientation, 19
distance, 32, 43
distortion, 5, 62–64
distraction, 8, 196
distress, 67, 68
diversity, 22, 69, 72, 79
divide, 41, 42, 158
documentation, 156
duality, 45
dynamic, 151, 153, 161, 169, 178, 185

ecosystem, 193
education, 2, 3, 5, 10–12, 15, 19, 29, 76, 79, 81, 91–96, 103–109, 114, 117,

122–124, 150, 163, 164, 167–169, 172, 174–180, 182–185, 189–194, 205
educator, 87
Edward Hall's, 43
effectiveness, 2, 13, 90, 92, 95, 102, 103, 109, 110, 119, 129, 134, 158, 181, 182, 190, 193, 195, 200
efficacy, 121, 213
effort, 69
empathy, 17, 19, 43, 44, 46, 47, 49, 65, 66, 68, 103, 104, 137, 185
employee, 54
empowerment, 76
encryption, 20
energy, 143, 185
engagement, 8, 49, 62, 76, 93, 98, 102, 141, 143, 147, 152, 153, 157, 159, 161, 169, 177, 182, 192, 194, 200, 202, 214, 217, 220
enhancement, 147
enjoyment, 157
entertainment, 3, 5–7, 10, 143, 145, 163, 164
environment, 2, 8, 56, 59, 63, 67, 68, 78, 101–103, 108, 114, 129, 133, 136, 146, 150, 153, 157, 192, 205, 207, 209
equality, 72–74
equation, 6, 7, 91, 101, 103, 108, 117, 143, 158, 185, 194, 200, 203
equipment, 41, 128, 147
equity, 42, 79
era, 141, 153

escape, 68
escapism, 36
establishment, 70
event, 68
evolution, 5, 10, 52
example, 7, 16, 20, 21, 41, 56, 68, 105, 137, 146, 193
exchange, 16, 17, 43, 44, 104
excitement, 152
experience, 4, 6, 8, 9, 20, 25, 27, 43, 45, 56, 66, 72, 87, 91, 101, 102, 104, 106, 114, 124, 135, 143, 146, 147, 150, 152, 153, 157, 158, 164, 173, 182, 187, 191–193, 203, 212, 220
experiment, 101, 146, 187
experimentation, 102, 114
exploitation, 21, 66
exploration, 3, 106, 145
exposure, 2, 21, 66, 67, 129, 171, 182, 207, 222
expression, 157
extent, 56
eye, 17, 27

face, 103, 105, 136, 170
facility, 217
faculty, 191
fan, 147
fear, 7, 63, 66, 207
feedback, 2, 8, 17, 56, 91, 101, 103, 117, 159, 161, 187
feeling, 63
fidelity, 2
field, 41, 72, 100, 101, 105, 129, 152, 158, 200, 202
film, 139–141
filmmaking, 140

fitness, 56
flight, 2
flow, 157
flying, 63
focus, 33, 71, 74, 79, 111, 196
food, 105
force, 7, 47, 74
forest, 193
formation, 32
foster, 33, 47, 66, 101, 103, 153, 161, 177, 185, 194
frame, 152, 158
frontier, 10, 17
function, 91
future, 3, 9, 10, 23–25, 39, 42, 52, 54, 59, 71, 72, 91, 93, 96, 98, 103, 108, 111, 114, 117, 119, 124, 132, 141, 143, 145, 148, 151, 152, 156, 159, 161, 174, 177, 182, 185, 187, 191, 200, 202, 205, 214, 219, 222

gain, 21, 203
game, 68, 146, 147, 152, 157, 159
gameplay, 5, 55, 68
gaming, 5, 6, 8–10, 16, 20, 21, 55, 157–159
gap, 105, 191
Geert Hofstede's, 43
gender, 22, 72–74
generation, 108, 117, 169, 194
gimmick, 102
good, 47, 79
growth, 93, 151, 159

habitat, 193
hacking, 20
Hall, 43

hand, 17
harassment, 20, 78
hardware, 9, 102, 152, 158
harm, 67, 68
hassle, 147
headset, 136
healing, 200
health, 15, 19, 21, 41, 56, 64, 117–119, 145, 151, 197–200, 220
healthcare, 3, 5, 13–15, 41, 66, 125, 132, 136–138, 191, 197, 210, 212, 217–220, 222
hinge, 145
history, 3, 98, 173, 175–178
hope, 200
horizon, 132
horror, 7
hospital, 135
host, 16
hub, 16

identity, 20, 56, 63
imbalance, 22
imitation, 104
ImmerseMe, 105
immersion, 6, 8, 139, 150, 152, 157, 159, 161, 164
impact, 3, 7, 21, 22, 33, 42, 47, 49, 64, 67, 74, 148, 150, 158
imperative, 22, 42, 56, 62, 72, 76, 79
implementation, 11, 54, 91, 95, 102, 103, 106–108, 119, 121, 122, 132, 135, 138, 142, 168, 169, 172, 174, 178, 180, 185–187, 196, 198, 204, 205, 214, 217
importance, 45, 56, 58, 59, 101–104, 114, 117, 192, 203

improvement, 117, 182
inclusion, 79
inclusivity, 17, 22, 42, 54, 69, 76, 158
income, 41
incorporation, 191, 210
increase, 106, 147, 159, 182, 193
independence, 93
individual, 119, 122, 129, 161, 180, 202, 207, 220
individualism, 43
industry, 5, 7, 9, 10, 21, 22, 56, 72, 74, 76, 140, 141, 147, 150, 159
infancy, 150
information, 20, 55, 56, 147
ingenuity, 5
initiative, 193
injury, 146
innovation, 3, 7, 56, 71, 72, 129, 147
input, 8
instance, 6, 17, 20, 21, 55, 63, 67, 68, 136, 146, 147, 173, 182
instruction, 103
integration, 8, 10, 14, 16, 39, 40, 51, 54, 57, 76, 78, 82, 87, 96, 97, 101–104, 106, 107, 109, 111, 113, 114, 117–119, 122, 123, 139, 142–145, 147, 150, 153, 161, 167, 171, 174, 177, 183, 186, 191, 193, 194, 196, 200, 203, 205, 212, 214, 217, 220–222
integrity, 57
intelligence, 17, 159, 161
intention, 67
interaction, 3, 10, 16, 17, 31, 36, 39, 52, 62, 137, 143, 192, 217
interactivity, 139, 153

interest, 3
interface, 3, 202
interplay, 10
intersection, 36, 151, 153, 222
introduction, 3
investment, 3, 102, 106
isolation, 16
issue, 22, 67, 147

Jon Kabat-Zinn, 133
journey, 3, 148

kitchen, 187
knee, 146
knowledge, 82, 101, 104, 106, 108, 191, 192, 203
Kolb, 101, 104, 106, 114, 192

lack, 21, 22, 55, 72, 171
landscape, 6, 15, 17, 52, 69, 71, 72, 111, 132, 138, 145, 147, 157, 159, 222
language, 27, 94–96, 105, 169–172
latency, 158
learning, 10, 12, 40, 41, 65, 66, 78, 81–83, 86, 87, 91–94, 96, 98, 101–106, 108, 114, 117, 122, 124, 161, 169–173, 176, 178, 180, 182, 184, 185, 187, 189–192, 194, 203, 205
lens, 8, 43, 57, 67
Leonardo da Vinci, 173
level, 41, 147
leverage, 90
life, 5, 21, 54, 68, 72, 101, 105, 119, 193, 217
line, 147
literacy, 42, 138
literature, 31

Index

location, 152, 153
London, 77
loneliness, 16, 35, 36
look, 52
loyalty, 147

machine, 78, 161
maintenance, 32, 102
making, 17, 72, 98, 106, 114, 145–147, 152, 157
management, 5, 14, 41, 102, 103, 109–111, 195–197, 214, 222
manipulation, 5, 7, 17, 20, 64–66, 68, 69, 73
manner, 5, 105
marketing, 56, 68
mass, 143, 185
material, 105
measure, 158
media, 16, 21, 27, 38–40, 45, 47
medicine, 191, 220–222
meditation, 135
medium, 5, 7, 72, 135, 161, 220
messaging, 68
metaphor, 143
method, 146
Michelangelo, 173
Mihaly Csikszentmihalyi, 157
mind, 22
mindfulness, 133–135
miscommunication, 29
misuse, 20, 55, 56
mobility, 16
model, 106, 220
modeling, 102, 104
module, 182
moment, 133
morality, 67

Morton Heilig, 3
motion, 2, 3, 6, 129, 146, 152, 158
motivation, 122
motor, 122
movement, 146
multitude, 101
music, 148–151

narrative, 22, 152
nature, 2, 45, 56, 59, 68, 152, 156
necessity, 70
need, 21, 69, 72, 87, 102, 137, 147, 187
neglect, 68
New York, 77

object, 207
obligation, 68
observation, 102, 114
offering, 15, 17, 44, 49, 68, 93, 101, 105, 111, 114, 129, 141, 159, 180, 194, 197, 200, 212
one, 16, 56, 63
opportunity, 74, 87, 96, 101, 147, 153, 185, 191, 209, 217
other, 17, 56, 105, 147
outcome, 63
over, 21, 56, 147
overfishing, 193
overload, 157
oversight, 21

pacing, 152
pain, 5, 14, 41, 109–111, 195–197, 214, 222
part, 152
participation, 68, 72, 203
past, 178

patient, 14, 15, 63, 111, 117, 122, 132, 136, 137, 191, 196, 197, 200, 202, 207, 210–212, 214, 220, 222
pedagogy, 124, 177
peer, 102
perception, 64, 196
perform, 146
performance, 56, 101, 114, 147, 150, 187
person, 45
perspective, 25, 45, 147
phenomenon, 20, 56, 60, 63
philosophy, 67, 133
phobia, 128, 129, 207, 209, 210
physics, 143, 185
pilot, 182
pioneer, 133
place, 137
planet, 194
platform, 16, 20, 56, 69, 102–106, 117, 150
play, 44, 52, 69, 73, 135, 146, 220
player, 8, 157, 159
pollution, 193
portrayal, 73
potential, 2, 3, 5, 7–12, 15–18, 20–22, 25, 29, 32, 33, 35, 36, 38, 42–44, 47, 49, 51–56, 60, 62–64, 67–69, 73, 76, 79, 83, 86, 87, 90–93, 95–98, 100–104, 106–108, 111, 113, 114, 117, 118, 121, 122, 125, 129, 131, 132, 134–138, 140–145, 147, 149, 150, 152, 153, 157–161, 164, 168, 169, 172–174, 176–178, 180–182, 184–187, 190, 192, 193, 196–198, 200, 202, 205, 209–213, 218–220
power, 21, 25, 33, 43, 66, 108, 160, 169
practice, 2, 101, 102, 104, 105, 111, 114, 117, 137, 146, 171, 182, 187, 203
premise, 207
presence, 6, 8, 27, 31, 45, 133, 139, 157
present, 133, 217
preservation, 156, 157
pressure, 146
principle, 55
privacy, 2, 5, 17, 20, 22, 33, 40, 54, 56, 59, 67–69, 71, 147
process, 68, 101, 106, 129, 192, 208
processing, 2, 3, 129
production, 152
profit, 21
program, 103, 105, 135, 182
progress, 2
project, 193
promise, 46, 98, 105, 119, 129, 138, 146, 161, 178, 194, 196, 212, 222
promotion, 22
provider, 137
psychologist, 157
psychology, 133
purpose, 66, 133

quality, 33, 103, 119, 152, 158, 177, 194, 217
quest, 3

race, 63
rainforest, 193

Index   231

range, 5, 55, 74, 102, 146
rate, 152, 158
reach, 149, 200
readiness, 146
reading, 146
realism, 17
reality, 2–5, 8–10, 16, 17, 19, 21, 31,
    33, 36, 40, 42, 50–52, 56,
    62–64, 70–72, 74, 76,
    117, 135, 143, 147, 148,
    150, 151, 153, 157, 159,
    196, 214
realm, 185
recovery, 146, 200
reduction, 135, 207, 222
reflection, 91, 114, 203
refugee, 105
regulation, 21, 69–72, 212
rehabilitation, 5, 15, 113, 114, 122,
    146, 147, 201, 202, 214
relation, 5
relationship, 17, 32, 35, 103, 108,
    117, 148
reliance, 147
relief, 68, 111, 197
reminder, 3, 101
remote, 136, 218–220
report, 182
representation, 22, 44, 49, 69, 72,
    74, 79
requirement, 152
research, 12, 33, 74, 79, 111, 114,
    119, 129, 132, 182, 196,
    200, 202, 214, 219, 222
resolution, 158
resonance, 45
resource, 3, 105
responsibility, 7, 22, 68
restaurant, 105

restructuring, 196
result, 68, 114
resurgence, 3
retention, 96, 104, 106, 203
return, 146
review, 31
revolution, 25
richness, 27
rise, 2, 61, 66
risk, 21, 59, 102, 114, 115, 146
role, 44, 49, 52, 69, 71–73, 117, 135,
    146, 164, 212, 220
row, 147

safety, 59, 63, 69, 71, 129
San Francisco, 135
satisfaction, 8, 153, 157
scalability, 128
scenario, 137, 207
scrutiny, 56
sea, 193
second, 146
section, 182
security, 2, 20, 22, 56–59, 68, 69
sensation, 157
sense, 6, 16, 27, 45
sensitivity, 21, 105
service, 56
session, 67
set, 6
setting, 135, 146, 150, 203
severity, 129
share, 16, 17, 55, 56
shift, 145, 152, 157
shooting, 146
show, 129, 182
sickness, 129, 152, 158
significance, 173
simulation, 68, 103, 114, 137

situation, 207
skill, 90, 91, 117, 146, 187
socialization, 17
society, 22, 25, 47, 61, 64, 69, 71, 74
software, 9, 102, 147, 158
sound, 66
space, 16, 17, 21, 101, 104, 147, 158
specialist, 136
spectator, 147
spirit, 3, 141
staple, 202
state, 5, 8, 152, 157
stewardship, 194
storyline, 153
storytelling, 5, 49, 72, 141, 153, 160, 161
strain, 146
strategy, 182
strength, 146
stress, 135, 222
structure, 43
struggle, 16, 21, 41
student, 169
studio, 173
study, 63, 66, 135, 174, 205
subject, 21
success, 152
suit, 152
suitability, 196
summary, 69
superficiality, 36
support, 16, 102, 200, 217–220
surface, 2
surgery, 135
surrounding, 7, 33, 69
sustainability, 129

target, 55, 56
teacher, 96, 101–103, 180–182
teaching, 101–103, 182
technique, 63, 146
technology, 2, 3, 5–7, 9, 10, 15, 17, 19, 22, 23, 29, 33, 41, 42, 44, 47, 49, 51, 52, 54, 56, 59, 62, 64, 66, 69, 71, 73, 74, 79, 87, 91, 93, 96, 98, 100–103, 106, 108, 109, 111, 114, 115, 117, 119, 122, 124, 125, 128, 132, 138, 141, 143, 145, 147, 148, 151–153, 157–159, 161, 162, 164, 169–172, 174, 177, 178, 180, 182, 185, 187, 191, 194, 197, 200, 202, 204, 205, 209, 210, 212, 214, 217, 220, 222
telecommunications, 210
telehealth, 217, 218, 220
telemedicine, 130–132, 210–212
television, 152, 153
term, 33, 74, 79, 129, 202
testament, 5
the Oculus Rift, 3, 6
theft, 20, 56
theme, 144, 145
theory, 43, 72, 81, 91, 101, 114, 139, 157, 192
therapy, 19, 29, 66, 67, 114, 120–122, 129, 163, 200, 207, 213, 214, 222
threat, 63
throw, 146
time, 2, 20, 68, 78, 102, 153, 161, 194
tool, 3, 5, 33, 47, 49, 68, 69, 74, 76, 79, 93, 102, 135, 191, 222
tracking, 3, 6, 17

Index

traction, 2
traffic, 147
trainee, 101, 102
training, 2, 5, 14, 15, 54, 79, 87, 96, 101–103, 114–117, 123, 125, 133, 134, 137, 146, 147, 180–182, 186, 187, 191, 203–205, 222
trajectory, 108
transformation, 101, 104, 106, 153, 185
transparency, 55, 56
treatment, 14, 15, 117–119, 128, 129, 196–201, 207, 209, 210, 212
triad, 57
trust, 56, 59

uncertainty, 43
understanding, 3, 5, 10, 17, 33, 40, 43–45, 47, 56, 59, 63, 64, 68, 72, 74, 79, 101, 103–106, 129, 137, 169, 173, 174, 177, 193, 194, 203
university, 103
unpredictability, 147
usage, 21, 68
use, 2, 5, 10, 36, 47, 48, 69, 73, 81, 94, 105, 111, 116–118, 122, 129, 135, 140, 146, 147, 169, 175, 179, 184, 185, 187, 189, 192, 197, 198, 220

user, 2–4, 6, 9, 20, 21, 39, 40, 55, 56, 59, 67, 69, 71, 143, 152, 158, 159, 161, 202

validation, 212
variability, 122, 202
vehicle, 73, 79
view, 152, 158
viewer, 153
viewership, 147
viewing, 152, 153
violence, 21
visual, 8, 150, 158
voice, 56
VR, 58, 63

way, 4, 12, 14, 87, 96, 122, 132, 133, 141, 143, 145, 147, 151, 153, 159, 164, 169, 171, 172, 174, 178, 185, 197, 200, 210, 212
weather, 193
welfare, 21
well, 33, 41, 54, 69, 135, 145, 174, 191, 214, 217
wellness, 220
work, 40, 54, 62, 64, 108
workforce, 187
workplace, 53, 54
world, 5, 13, 16, 20, 21, 25, 27, 33, 62, 63, 68, 101, 104, 105, 108, 135, 157, 169, 171, 185, 192